100 THINGS TO DO IN BILLINGS BEFORE YOU DIE

Bighorn Canyon

100 THINGS TO DO IN BILLINGS BEFORE YOU DIE

NANCY ICOPINI AND GINA TARNACKI

Reedy Press
PO Box 5131
St. Louis, MO 63139, USA
www.reedypress.com

Library of Congress Control Number: 2023938647

ISBN: 9781681064536

Design by Jill Halpin

All photos are by the authors unless otherwise noted.

Printed in the United States of America
23 24 25 26 27   5 4 3 2 1

DEDICATION

To my husband and daughters who bring so much joy to my life and are always up for a road trip and adventures in Montana. And to "the farm."—Gina

To my children, Gina, Jacole, Angela, and Mitch, whose love of Montana warms my heart. And to my parents, Ernie and Marian, for exemplifying all that I value about Montana.—Nancy

Tippet Rise

CONTENTS

Sports and Recreation

Culture and History

Shopping and Fashion

PREFACE

Known as the Magic City because of the way the population exploded, seemingly overnight after the railroad came through, Billings has continued to create a magical place to live and play through a host of outdoor activities, cultural attractions, creative outlets, and those unforgettable views. One of my earliest memories of childhood is seeing the twinkling lights of the Billings cityscape when arriving from the north and driving down into the city from the top of the Rimrocks. Decades later that view still never gets old. I was born in Billings. Though I no longer live there, my mom, sister, and countless relatives still live in Billings so I frequently return, and now I have my own two young daughters in tow. Just like me, they're enchanted by the Rimrocks.

Another thing to love about Billings? Everyone's just so nice! When my mom (and cowriter), Nancy, retired and moved back to Billings after many years away, she joked that she had forgotten that she needs to add extra buffer time to all her errands because of all the friendly people working at the cash registers or just walking through the store who are constantly striking up conversations. That really sums up Billings: it's a city with a small-town heart.

That's not to say Billings doesn't have some cosmopolitan aspects to offer, though. Over the past decade, we've enjoyed watching Billings grow, especially in the music, arts, and culinary categories. The brewery scene in Billings is one of the best in the nation in our opinion, especially thanks to the Brewery Walking Trail. Murals and theater and the craftsmanship of western wear are also on full display in Billings. You'll find a host of excellent and diverse places to eat all around the city. Which is good since with so many outdoor adventures in and near Billings, you're bound to work up an appetite.

After all, Billings is called "Montana's Trailhead" because it's the perfect base from which to explore so many natural areas. Fly fish the Yellowstone, hike or bike one of the many trails, raft down the Stillwater, go skiing in Red Lodge, drive the Beartooth Highway, reflect on history where the battle of the Little Bighorn took place. Whatever your interest, easy day trips from Billings abound.

When compiling this list we consulted many friends and family members for their input, stopped in and spoke with business owners, and explored places again that we hadn't been to in awhile. We wanted to find the things that make Billings . . . well, *Billings*. Things that would really give you the aura of what this city we love is all about. It was hard to narrow it down to just 100, reminding us why we truly believe Billings is the next destination hot spot in the USA. Whether you're coming from near or far to explore Billings, we think you'll enjoy this list of things to do and discover aspects of Billings and the surrounding region you never knew existed.

Red Lodge Mountain

ACKNOWLEDGMENTS

Thank you to our friends and family who helped us discover hidden gems and narrow down our list of things to do in Billings, especially Kris Carpenter, Coleen and Kenny Lind, Kayla Mershon, and Todd Icopini. Thanks to Angela Babcock for her lovely photography. In addition, we thank all of the visitor and wildlife bureaus in Montana who work hard to educate visitors to "Recreate Responsibly." You can learn more about how to recreate responsibly here: fwp.mt.gov/stateparks/recreate-responsibly.

We also appreciate all of the local business owners and employees who strive to provide so many wonderful activities and experiences in and around Billings.

Finally, we would like to acknowledge the Crow, Northern Cheyenne, Sioux, and Blackfeet peoples on whose ancestral lands Billings now sits.

Sassy Biscuit

FOOD AND DRINK

1

BRUNCH WITH SOUTHERN FLAIR
AT THE SASSY BISCUIT CO.

Waffle biscuits and cookie butter await you at the Sassy Biscuit, which brings a southern flair to brunching in Billings. These are not your ordinary brunch dishes (you'll even find grits and collards as options!) thanks in part to the owner's degree in culinary arts, which shines through each dish. In addition to the decadent waffle biscuits, savory biscuit sammie sandwiches and creatively prepared porridge dishes are also available. The dishes have a homemade flair, from the biscuits made from scratch each morning to the house smoked bacon. Weekend brunches are especially popular at the Sassy Biscuit due to the unlimited mimosas. The Sassy Biscuit tends to be a busy and popular place. The line to order at the counter typically goes quickly, though, and the tables usually turn over by the time your food arrives. While you wait, you can enjoy the eclectic farmhouse decor of the restaurant.

115 N 29th St., 406-200-7530
thesassybiscuit.com

OTHER BREAKFAST SPOTS

Bernie's Diner
Choices of light menu options to hearty, full breakfasts.

Northern Hotel
19 N Broadway
406-867-6773
northernhotel.com

Great Harvest Bread of Billings
Muffins, scones, and cinnamon rolls in addition to bread baked fresh daily. Outside patio and indoor seating.

907 Poly Dr.
406-248-8889
3133 Central Ave.
406-702-1505
greatharvestbillings.com

McCormick Café
Freshly baked breakfast rolls and large popular omelets.

2419 Montana Ave.
406-255-9555
mccormickcafe.com

PAYS Cafe
Homestyle breakfasts.

1802 Minnesota Ave.
406-252-3034
facebook.com/
payscafeandcatering

Sophie's Kitchen
Delicious and interesting combinations in breakfast dishes.

Shiloh Commons
149 Shiloh Rd.
406-702-2022
sophieskitchenbillings.com

Stella's Kitchen and Bakery
Famous for their giant cinnamon rolls.

2525 1st Ave. N
406-248-3060
stellaskitchenandbakery.com

Tippy Cow Cafe
Large breakfast menu, more than 30 items.

279 E Airport Rd.
406-534-3599
facebook.com/tippycowcafe

Veronika's Pastry Shop
James Beard Outstanding Pastry Chef semifinalist specializing in European and Russian pastries.

2513 Montana Ave.
406-855-5770
facebook.com/
veronikaspastryshop

2

SAVOR THE BEST STROOPWAFEL AROUND

AT CARAMEL COOKIE WAFFLES

Gooey goodness awaits you at Caramel Cookie Waffles, a local eatery known for its authentic stroopwafels. The Dutch delicacy of drizzling caramel in between two thin waffle cookies may be an old tradition in the Netherlands, but it's harder to find them perfectly made in the states. At Caramel Cookie Waffles, they get it right with an airy softness to the stroopwafel cookie that crumbles in your mouth amid caramel that isn't hard or overly sticky. So how'd Billings get so lucky to be the home for these yummy treats? Owner Jan Boogman is from the Netherlands. He met his future wife, Judy, when she visited the Netherlands as a University of Montana athlete. They moved to Billings and started Caramel Cookie Waffles in 1987. Jan and Judy still run the business and have many loyal customers who come into their cozy café for a light breakfast or lunch and stroopwafels. You can even watch the stroopwafels being made while you wait at the counter.

1707 17th St. W, 406-252-1960
caramelcookiewaffles.com

3

CATCH A FLYING BURGER
AT KING'S HAT DRIVE-IN

OK, you don't actually have to catch your burger at the King's Hat, Billings's oldest drive-through. It's just what this beloved burger institution calls their signature sandwich. The "Flying Burger" consists of a slider-type burger patty placed between two pieces of white bread that are smashed together and crimped on the edges. The result? A flying saucer–looking sandwich. Ignore your inner voice telling you white bread is no good—bite in and you'll know why cars line up around the block all year long to order one of these tasty burgers. Don't forget to order the potato gems or onion rings as a side, and if you're not feeling like a burger, choose one of their other meat or fish sandwiches. The King's Hat also has fun drink options: the Bee Bop and the Hot-n-Tot. The Bee Bop will make you think you're day drinking, but this nonalcoholic rum-flavored cola won't get you in trouble. If you want a bit of a bite in your cola, try the cinnamon-flavored Hot-n-Tot.

105 S 37th St., 406-259-4746
facebook.com/profile.php?id=100040056895799

4

ENJOY AN ARTISAN COFFEE

AT BLACK DOG COFFEE HOUSE

We love a good latte or cappuccino, but when it comes to Black Dog Coffee House, "black" is the way to go. OK, maybe with a little cream and sugar. We're talking about Black Dog's specialty: a handcrafted pour-over coffee. This method of brewing coffee provides fresher, more flavorful mugs of java, and Black Dog is an expert at it.

Priding itself as a conscientious third-wave neighborhood coffee shop, Black Dog keeps things local with its coffee beans, too. Coffee beans are sourced from artisan roasters, including Revel, a local roaster who roasts the coffee beans to Black Dog's specifications for just the right flavor notes.

Whether you sit and savor a cup of coffee here in the morning or as an alternative to a "happy hour" drink in the afternoon, you will appreciate the attention and care the staff has put into its preparation.

Three Black Dog Coffee Houses are located around Billings.

The Original Black Dog: 1528 24th St. W, 406-534-8822
Black Dog at Roots Garden Center: 2147 Poly Dr., 406-690-8979
Black Dog on 10th Ave.: 3115 10th Ave. N, 406-281-8550
blackdogcoffeehouse.com

5

DEVOUR HANDCRAFTED SWEETS

AT BROCKEL'S CHOCOLATES

If you love gourmet, artisan-crafted chocolate, you can't miss out on experiencing the sweets at Brockel's Chocolates. It's the place to go for chocolate in Billings—expect a long line in the days leading up to Valentine's Day! You'll be supporting a local business as this chocolateria is a family affair, with three generations of the Brockel family getting involved in the making of the treats. Some of those sweet delights are even named after the owner's daughters (who also help run the shop) and grandchildren. The Brockels opened up their shop over four decades ago and it retains its friendly "mom-and-pop store" vibe to this day as the chocolates are still handcrafted following their own family recipes. In addition to a variety of chocolate and fudge, you'll find candy apples, double-dipped ice cream bars, kettle corn, and even chocolate-covered strawberries for special occasions.

117 N 29th St., 406-248-2705
facebook.com/brockelschocolatesmt

6

TOUR AN AQUAPONICS GREENHOUSE RUN BY KOI FISH

Tour Swanky Roots and take home some fresh greens for dinner, grown using aquaponics. Swanky Roots is run by a mother-daughter duo who are thrilled to share this new way of farming with people. Aquaponics is made possible by on-site koi ponds. The waste from the fish create the necessary fertilizer needed for the plants, while any leftover water from the plants gets returned to the fish. In turn, water is greatly conserved and the plants get all the nutrients they need, resulting in faster growth and lasting freshness. Swanky Roots is passionate about educating others about this innovative type of agriculture and offers tours of the facility, which sits on 60 acres on the western edge of Billings. During the tour, you'll learn more about the process, see the fishponds, and view where the vegetables are grown.

8333 Story Rd., 406-656-7668
swankyroots.com

TIP

No time to schedule a tour? You can also visit the storefront at the facility to purchase the greenhouse veggies and herbs. Aquaponics enables leafy vegetables like lettuce, kale, Swiss chard, and sprouts to be grown year-round. Additionally, herbs like mint and basil are grown within the walls of this unique greenhouse. Beef from the owners' farm is also available along with other Montana-made food products.

7

WALK
THE BILLINGS BREW TRAIL

If you love an exquisite pint of craft beer, Montana's the place for you. Did you know, though, that Montana's only walkable brewery trail is located right in downtown Billings? Convenience combined with fun and tastiness await. Many of the tasting rooms have views of the beer-making equipment, including fermentation barrels. The Billings Brew Trail is 1.5 miles long through downtown Billings. The Billings Visitor Center makes it even easier for you to experience these breweries thanks to its helpful brew trail map on its website. It details all the breweries and taprooms, plus a distillery to check out. Also register for the Billing Brew Trail Pass. It's free and easy to use; no app required! At each participating brewery, ask the bartender or other staff member to provide the dedicated PIN number. Plug it in and get a check-in badge for that brewery and possibly a discount. A certain number of check-ins qualifies you to redeem your pass for a prize (such as a sticker, T-shirt, or souvenir glass) from Visit Billings.

visitbillings.com/billings-brew-trail

STOPS ALONG THE WALKABLE BREW TRAIL

Thirsty Street at the Garage
2123 1st Ave. N

Last Chance Pub and Cider Mill
2203 Montana Ave.

Asylum Distillery
2223 Montana Ave.

Uberbrew
2305 Montana Ave.

Carter's Brewing
2526 Montana Ave.

Angry Hank's Microbrewery
20 N 30th St.

Thirsty Street Brewing Company Tap Room & Bottle Shop
3008 1st Ave. N

Montana Brewing Company
113 N Broadway

8

DIVE INTO AN AWARD-WINNING BURGER

AT THE BURGER DIVE

The Burger Dive has many accolades yet it has stayed unpretentious and feels just like a chill neighborhood burger joint should. Checkered floors, friendly service, and an order counter await you when you step inside to enjoy Billings's must-try hamburger. This downtown Billings eatery sources its ingredients locally as much as possible. Even its buns are made by Grains of Montana. The Burger Dive's award-winning burgers have taken top prizes at the Taste of Billings, Masters of the Barbecue Challenge, Food Network South Beach Wine and Food Festival Burger Bash, and even the popular televised World Food Championship. The winner for that last one is the "I'm Your Huckleberry Burger," the must-try burger at this joint. Layered atop the Angus beef patty are bacon, goat cheese, roasted red pepper mayo, arugula, and the kicker: Brad's Huckleberry Hatch chili barbecue sauce. Who's Brad? He's the head chef and owner of the Burger Dive, who runs it alongside his family.

114 N 27th St., 406-281-8292
theburgerdive.com

9

WELCOME SUMMER
WITH A CONE FROM SOFTIES

You know summer is just around the corner when Softies opens up again, as it has been doing for decades. With a nostalgic flair, Softies will have you feeling like a kid—and have your kids begging to go. You won't find hot eats on this menu, just chilly treats. Soft-serve ice cream is king here and can be ordered plain or as one of their three specialties: Dip, Flavor Burst, or Bliz-its for the cookie and candy monsters in your group. If you're not in the mood for a creamy treat, get one of the fruit smoothies or slushies. Frozen yogurt, shakes, sundaes, snow cones, and frozen bananas are also on the menu. Expect a line on hot summer days—but it's worth the wait once you have that cold treat in your hand.

2407 Broadwater Ave., 406-702-1523
facebook.com/softies406

10

ORDER THE WILD GAME SAMPLER
AT BUFFALO BLOCK

The rich, warm wood paneling and soft lighting make Buffalo Block a popular spot for a romantic dinner. And what could be more romantic than nibbling on rattlesnake and rabbit sausage with your special someone? OK, even if that's not your idea of romance, you're still in for an amazing meal at this popular downtown Billings restaurant known for its superb dry-aged beef. Up the fun with an order of the Wild Game Sampler. You'll get to sample grilled elk filet, quail, bison bone marrow, venison sausage, and yes, rattlesnake and rabbit sausage—all wild game found in Montana. The swanky bar area also mixes up some delicious cocktails featuring local spirits. Enjoy your drinks and food inside the rustic chic dining room or on the large outdoor patio, which sometimes plays host to live music on warm summer nights.

2401 Montana Ave., 406-245-7477
buffaloblock.com

11

LEARN FROM A LOCAL CHEF

AT ZEST

Get the insider view of the culinary scene in Billings and learn some terrific new cooking skills at Zest. Locally owned, Zest is a place for both retail and classes. Cooking classes range from truffle creating to sushi rolling to pasta making and so much more. There are even kitchen utensil skill classes like Knife 101, where you learn how to properly use a kitchen knife and which kind to use for different prep styles. If you need to purchase some equipment to continue your cooking at home, the retail side of Zest has just about any type of kitchen tool you'll need. We also recommend picking up some fresh pasta by Seconde in the refrigerated cooler and if you love it like we do, check for Seconde chef Lisa's pasta making classes on the Zest calendar.

110 N 29th St., 406-534-8427
zestbillings.com

12

SIP WORLD-CLASS WINE
AT CITY VINEYARD

Montana isn't typically known for wine tasting, but City Vineyard in Billings is looking to change that. The 5,000-square-foot space sells wines from all over the world, with more than 10,000 bottles within the store. City Vineyard has been in Billings since 2000 and has moved into larger spaces multiple times since opening. City Vineyard is a great place to find the perfect vintage of wine to take home, but we like it even more because it's a destination unto itself: adjoining the retail space is their popular wine bar where wine tasting is offered alongside savory tapas. The wine menu is frequently rotating with more than two dozen wines on the menu. Order by the glass or try a tasting flight. Limited indoor and outdoor seating is available.

1335 Golden Valley Circle, 406-867-1491
cityvineyardwine.com

TIP

For a special experience at City Vineyard, check their website for wine tasting and food pairing events. City Vineyard brings in representatives from wineries around the world to share their knowledge about the wines being presented.

13

MEET FOR A MARTINI
AT DOC HARPER'S

The doctor called . . . and prescribed a martini. OK, that's only the case if the doctor in question is Doc Harper, aka Doc Harper's Tavern. This local bar is named after the owner's father, Robert Dana Harper, who was a country doctor in southeast Montana from the 1930s to the 1970s. He also loved martinis, and his legacy continues at this swanky bar in downtown Billings that serves up some of the best martinis in the state. Doc Harper's Tavern is lined with a bar on one side where you can take a seat and watch the mixologists at work. A smattering of tables line the other wall. Whichever side you pick, you won't be far away from the other—this watering hole is only 18 feet wide, which gives it an almost speakeasy feel. Doc Harper's specialties are martinis with over 35 different martini options on the menu. Not sure what to order? Start with the spicy pickle martini, which is Doc Harper's most ordered drink.

116 N Broadway, 406-200-7177
docharpers.com

GO
ON AN INTERNATIONAL FOOD TOUR

Billings isn't just about steak and burgers. It has a burgeoning food scene that is rapidly growing in diversity with internationally inspired cuisine. To experience all these different tastes, we recommend checking out these five world-class restaurants:

The Athenian Greek Restaurant: Owned by three Greek brothers who create dishes using family recipes. Many of the spices, olive oil, feta, and other ingredients are imported from Greece. 18 N 29th St., 406-248-5681

Camacho's Tacos Mexican Restaurant: The place for authentic Mexican food in Billings with tacos, carne asada, chilaquiles, enchiladas, ceviches, and more. 2240 Grand Ave., 406-371-7109

Carverss Brazilian Steakhouse: Operated by a family with roots in both Brazil and Montana, Carverss has family-style dining featuring meat cooked churrasco-style over an open flame and then carved table-side. 1390 S 24th St. W, 406-200-7910

NaRa Restaurant for Sushi: An excellent sushi restaurant that specializes in fresh seafood and large specialty rolls. 3 Custer Ave., 406-245-8866

Siam Thai Restaurant: Delicious Thai food favorites are served here, including curry, phad thai, satay, and more. 3210 Henesta Dr., Ste. G, 406-652-4315

OTHER TOP-RATED PLACES TO EAT

Bistro Enzo
Mouthwatering seafood and pasta dishes, also steaks and wood-fired pizzas.

1502 Rehberg Ln.
406-651-0999
bistroenzo.com

Blues BBQ
Consistently voted the best barbeque spot in Billings. They also cater for events, large and small.

523 Hilltop Rd.
406-245-2583
bluesbbqbillings.com

Copper Onion Bistro
Distinctive dishes with incredible flavor combinations and craft cocktails.

115 Shiloh Rd.
406-254-1882
copperonionbistro.com

Juliano's Restaurant
Located in a former stable house, Juliano's has character and delicious food. It is a popular spot for a special dinner.

2912 7th Ave. N
406-248-6400
julianosrestaurant.com

The Montana Club
Extensive menu and great steakhouse. Go on your birthday to get a discount equal to your age.

1791 Majestic Ln.
406-969-1211
montanaclub.com

Walkers
Featuring Montana rainbow trout and other locally sourced food on their menu.

2700 1st Ave. N
406-245-9291
walkersgrill.com

15

SATISFY YOUR SWEET TOOTH

AT CANDY TOWN USA

You'll feel like you're in candy heaven as soon as you walk into Candy Town USA. You'll be wowed by the sheer size of it. Just about every type of candy imaginable is here, including hard-to-find favorites. Pick and choose your favorites and bag them up to purchase by weight. Select handcrafted chocolates, fudge, and candies from behind the long glass-fronted counter. Adding to the sweets euphoria is an old-fashioned soda fountain counter where you can order your favorite flavor as its bubbly self or served over ice cream, float style. Sundaes, milkshakes, and malts are also available. Need a gift? Candy Town USA has a variety of sweets-inspired gift baskets plus a Made in Montana section. One walk around this shop and you'll quickly see why it included "USA" in its name even though Billings is the only Candy Town location—but with more than 1,000 different candies available in one spot, why need more?

820 Shiloh Crossing, 406-651-9196
candytownusa.com

NO BULL— TRY THESE FRIES
AT THE EDGAR BAR

Bull Fries, that is. If you've never heard of this Montana delicacy that is commonly called Rocky Mountain oysters, well, you may be in for a surprise. They are, in fact, deep-fried slices of bull testicles. The Edgar Bar, a destination steakhouse in the small town of Edgar just 30 minutes from Billings, calls them Bull Fries and serves up some of the best around. Dip the crispy strip in the tangy sauce and nibble at it just to say you have tried one, or enjoy them alongside a beer. You'll notice a sign outside says "This Is Coors Country" to acknowledge the farmers in the area who produce barley for the Coors Brewing Company, so find a seat at the bar and enjoy a Coors with your Bull Fries. If you're quite certain this appetizer isn't for you, you're in luck. Edgar Bar knows how to do steaks better than most. They get them locally from Oswald Family Farms just down the road.

105 Elwell St., Edgar, 406-962-3091
edgarbarmontana.com

TIP

It is wise to make a reservation, regardless of the day or season; the place is usually filled during dinner hours.

17

TAKE A DRIVE
FOR AN INCREDIBLE MEAL

Driving to Red Lodge for an Italian meal is well worth it if your destination is the Piccola Cucina at Ox Pasture restaurant. You'll feel like you've been swept away to Sicily thanks to the dining room's "dolce vita" vibe. The aromas of homemade pasta and simmering sauces greet you as you enter the bustling, friendly restaurant. You'll likely hear Italian being spoken—and even sung, especially if there's an anniversary or birthday when all the patrons are encouraged to join in with song and dance! Piccola Cucina at Ox Pasture is a branch of the renowned Piccola Cucina restaurant group in New York City. Ox Pasture blends Montana roots with Sicilian culture thanks to Head Chef Benedetto (Benny) Bisacquino and Piccola Cucina Executive Chef Phillip Guardione. Chef Benny sources the beef and produces locally in Montana when possible for the Ox Pastures menu. Both chefs grew up in Sicily. Only open during the summer season; reservations are highly recommended.

7 Broadway Ave. N, Red Lodge, 406-446-1212
piccolacucinagroup.com/en/piccola-cucina-at-ox-pasture/

TIP

Order the Cacio e Pepe for the at-your-table fun of watching your server prep the pasta in a huge cheese wheel called "Caciocavallo."

OTHER DESTINATION RESTAURANTS

The Backporch
James Beard Best New Restaurant Semifinalist
Barbeque special recipes and slow-smoked meats, including their method of preparing pit beef.

101 Main St., Roundup
406-323-2100
thebackporchroundup.com

Black Canyon Bistro
Try the bison ribeye or elk medallions for a Montana treat.

116 Broadway Ave. S, Red Lodge
406-445-3245
blackcanyonbistro.com

Cafe Regis
Known for their delicious breakfast selections.

501 Word Ave. S, Red Lodge
406-446-1941
regiscafe.com

Greycliff Mill
An authentic water-powered gristmill where they grind the flour used in their bakery goods. Make a reservation for their biweekly Saturday gourmet farm-to-table dinner. The type of dinner is listed on their webpage.

11 Greycliff Creek Ln., Greycliff
406-930-0870
greycliffmill.com

Jersey Lilly
A truly Montana experience. The building is on the National Register of Historic Places and in the Cowboy Hall of Fame. Enjoy the beans and steak in the midst of local ranchers; there may even be horses tied up to the hitching post outside!

105 Main St., Ingomar
406-358-2278
facebook.com/pages/Jersey-Lilly/341323089226641

Prerogative Kitchen
James Beard Best Chef Semifinalist.
À la carte menu with delicious, superbly prepared small plates sure to please both carnivores and vegetarians.

104 Broadway Ave. S, Red Lodge
406-445-3232
prerogativekitchen.com

18

DINE WITH A VIEW
FROM 20 FLOORS UP

Billings doesn't have much in the way of skyscrapers. But that doesn't mean you can't still enjoy a bird's-eye view of the city with a cocktail or meal. Head to the 20th floor of the DoubleTree by Hilton Hotel in downtown Billings and you'll find the elegant Montana Sky Restaurant. This restaurant lives up to its name since you'll feel like you're dining in the sky thanks to its floor-to-ceiling windows that stretch along one side of the restaurant and provide incredible views of city lights and distant mountain ranges. Time your reservation for sunset so you can watch the sunlight beautifully fade behind the mountain horizon. Montana Sky is known for more than just its views though. The menu features sophisticated cuisine like New York strip steak, walleye, and maple-glazed pork chop. Get a side of the decadent English cheddar baked mac and cheese and a Montana-inspired cocktail from the bar menu to go with your entrée.

27 N 27th St., 406-252-7400
hilton.com/en/hotels/bildtdt-doubletree-billings/dining

Just looking for drinks in the sky with a laid-back ambiance? Check out 406 Kitchen & Tap Room. Its rooftop patio may only be one floor up instead of 20, but it still packs in a fun ambiance with a view. The patio serves up a wide variety of drinks plus a bar menu. The full menu is served below in the industrial-inspired dining room.

Babcock Theatre

MUSIC AND ENTERTAINMENT

19

MEET AT A FESTIVAL UNDER SKYPOINT
TO START AND END SUMMER

Skypoint is a sculpture built over an intersection downtown. It's a major landmark in downtown Billings and is often a meeting point. It's also where you can welcome in the agricultural season each year and then bid it goodbye thanks to the Strawberry Festival and HarvestFest. For over 30 years, the Strawberry Festival has been the largest street festival in Billings and celebrates the beginning of the summer season with food and entertainment in downtown Billings. Culinary and artisan vendors line the streets, stages play host to talented musicians and singers, a kid zone delights, and shopping abounds thanks to over 100 vendors. And of course, there are strawberries! Pallets upon pallets of strawberries and other fruit are brought in to sell at the festival. Get some to freeze to last you until HarvestFest, which marks the end of the season. HarvestFest, sponsored by Montana Brewing Company, is a bit smaller and has more of a focus on autumn fun, such as scarecrow contests, a beer garden with a pumpkin brew on tap, fall produce, and an overall "Oktoberfest" vibe.

Under Skypoint at N Broadway and 2nd Ave. N
downtownbillings.com/31st-strawberry-festival-montana
downtownbillings.com/the-18th-annual-downtown-harvestfest

OTHER FESTIVALS

St. Patrick's Day Parade and Celtic Fair
March, Saturday closest to St. Patrick's Day

Downtown, downtownbillings.com

Montana Renaissance Festival
First weekend in June

Red Lodge Rodeo Grounds, redlodge.com

SpringFest
June

Moss Mansion, 914 Division St., 406-256-5100
mossmansion.com

SummerFair
Last weekend in June

Yellowstone Art Museum, 401 N 27th St.
406-256-6804, artmuseum.org

Crazy Days Weekend
Last weekend in July

Downtown, downtownbillings.com

Big Sky International Balloon Rendezvous
July

Amend Park, bigskyballoonrally.com

Festival of Nations
August

Lions Park, Red Lodge, redlodge.com

Holiday Parade
Friday after Thanksgiving

Downtown, downtownbillings.com

WATCH A PERFORMANCE
IN THE "CROWN JEWEL OF DOWNTOWN BILLINGS"

The Alberta Bair Theater is called the "Crown Jewel of Downtown Billings." It's been the chosen venue in Billings for Tony Award–winning musicals, Grammy Award–winning artists, operas, and orchestras. The Alberta Bair Theater recently underwent a $13.9 million renovation and expansion. Today, the Alberta Bair Theater is better than ever while still showcasing its historic roots. In 1931, it was an art deco–inspired vaudeville and movie house called the Fox Theatre. By 1978 the theater was badly in need of repairs and plans were being made to transform it into a modern three-screen cinema. Luckily, a fundraiser saved the theater with a leading donation from Alberta Bair, a philanthropist who was born in the house that eventually became the base for the Fox Theatre.

2801 3rd Ave. N, 406-256-6052
albertabairtheater.org

TIP

Alberta Bair Theater's historic ambiance and acoustics make it one of the best places to attend concerts of the Billings Symphony Orchestra and Chorale. In June, enjoy the symphony's classical music at the annual Symphony in the Park, held at Pioneer Park
billingssymphony.org

GO EARLY, STAY LATE
AT MONTANAFAIR

It doesn't get much more Americana than walking around a local summer fair with food on a stick, trying your hand at winning a big stuffed animal, and going for a ride on the Ferris wheel. You'll find all that at MontanaFair plus animal and agricultural aspects that educate about the rural life of Montana. 4-H kids show off their animals and craftsmanship for the chance to win the top honors. Walk around the grounds of the fair (held each August at MetraPark) to see the cute farm animals and the hard work put into raising them. Sewing, cooking, arts, woodworking, and other life skills are also on display. Be sure to check out the stage lineup, which features top-name musicians, comedians, magicians, and of course, the rodeos. With so much to do and on display, it's easy to see how MontanaFair has become the largest event in the region with roughly 250,000 visitors attending each year.

308 6th Ave. N, 406-256-2400
montanafair.com

22

WATCH A FILM
AT THE HISTORIC BABCOCK THEATRE

The Babcock Theatre is the most glamorous spot in Billings to watch a movie. The impressive downtown building dates back to the early 1900s. After the original opera house burned down in 1906, local businessman Albert Babcock reimagined the space to be the premier place to watch a live performance (and eventually picture shows) west of the Mississippi. And indeed, people traveled hundreds of miles to watch a show in the "Jewel of the West." Today, the Babcock Theatre is a nonprofit event venue owned by the City of Billings. It underwent a major rehabilitation in 2012, transforming the theater back to its midcentury film viewing glory days. Tiered seating holds 750 people while the large screen is surrounded by gilded adornments. Movies are always changing and are run by Art House Billings. See new releases, indie films, classic movies, or attend one of the Nostalgia Nights showing popular films from the '80s or '90s—all while enjoying popcorn or even a glass of wine from the concession stand.

2812 2nd Ave. N, 406-534-1128
babcockbillings.com

TIP

Looking for a more modern, intimate atmosphere? In addition to managing the films for the Babcock Theatre, Art House Billings operates Art House Cinema and Pub downtown. This is the place to go for lesser-known artistic films, shown in a small screening room adjacent to a sleek bar. Independent, foreign, and low-budget films as well as documentaries are thoughtfully chosen to inspire musing and conversation. If you're a film buff around Billings in September, be sure to mark your calendar for the Montana International Film Festival (MINT), which shows films at both Babcock Theatre and Art House Cinema.

23

START THE WEEKEND EARLY

AT ALIVE AFTER 5

Forget Thirsty Thursday. In Billings it's all about Alive after 5 once summer rolls around. On Thursday nights from 5 p.m. to 9 p.m., get your weekend started early with some rollicking good music and drinks. Alive after 5 is a concert series held in downtown Billings each summer in collaboration with local businesses and musicians. A different Billings eatery, bar, or brewery hosts the band or solo musician each week. What makes this even more fun is that the concerts are held outside next to the hosting business. That part of the street is cordoned off to create the perfect alfresco event. Wristbands must be purchased for just a couple bucks if you are 21 or older and want to enjoy an alcoholic beverage (drinks are then extra); otherwise admission is free.

Downtown Billings
downtownbillings.com/events

TIP

A limited number of VIP tickets are available for those who want access to a special area with ice water, tables to sit at, and close proximity to one of the bars serving at the event.

ENJOY EASY OUTDOOR LISTENING

AT A ST. JOHN'S SUMMER CONCERT

Set up your lawn chair and listen to great music at the long-running St. John's Summer Concert Series. On Thursday evenings from mid-June to mid-August, free concerts are played in the Fred and Marie Miller Pavilion at St. John's United, an assisted senior living community in Billings. The concerts are open to the public and family-friendly if your kids can stay up a bit late. An opening act usually starts at 6 p.m. followed by the main musical act at 7 p.m. Local bands are often on the roster, though St. John's Summer Concert Series also has bands coming in from other locations around the country. Food trucks are on-site, but many guests bring their own food to have picnics on the grass while listening to the music under the warm evening sky.

3940 Rimrock Rd., 406-655-5600
facebook.com/stjohnsunitedevents

25

FOR YOUR LISTENING PLEASURE, SPEND AN EVENING

AT THE PUB STATION

When it's a live performance you're in the mood for, the place to go in Billings is The Pub Station. This happening spot doubles as a concert venue and tap house. Grab your friends or significant other and head here for an unforgettable night out filled with great acoustics and craft beer and cider. The Pub Station is also on the comedy circuit and it's a great place to see up-and-coming comedians. And if you're thinking beer and music will make you hungry, The Pub Station has you covered for that as well. Pie Guys Pizzeria is located right inside the venue and serves up pizzas by the whole pie or slice plus calzones, nachos, cheese bread, and salads. Popular performers sell out, so plan to buy your ticket in advance and not at the door. Shows usually start at 8 p.m. with doors opening at 7 p.m. on weekends.

2502 1st Ave. N, 406-894-2020
thepubstation.com

The Pub Station's tap room is also open for happy hour revelers with hours from 4 p.m. to 8 p.m. on Monday through Friday. This is a great time to check out The Pub Station when it's quieter and try some brews from new breweries. You can even pick up a growler filled with your favorite brew to take home.

DISCOVER UP-AND-COMING ARTISTS

AT CRAFT LOCAL

Craft Local is where you go to get discovered in Billings. This welcoming music venue hosts an open mic every Wednesday followed by a jam session. What makes this music venue even cooler is that it's a 501(c)(3) nonprofit that has the goal of promoting local musicians and artists. While there, walk around the gallery space and see more than 100 pieces of locally created art on display. The artwork is constantly changing so you never know if you'll discover your new favorite artist! Craft Local has been so popular that it outgrew its previous space and now resides on the first floor of the historic Hotel Carlin building. In addition to open mic nights, we also love Irish Music Tuesdays at Craft Local where you can listen to musicians perform tunes inspired by the Emerald Isle. While listening to music, you can sip on a craft beer, sourced from breweries all over Montana, and order a pizza or a few other yummy snacks served on-site.

2501 Montana Ave., 406-702-1458
craftlocal.org

DANCE THE COWBOY JITTERBUG

AT HIGH HORSE SALOON

Have you ever wanted to learn country western dances? Head on down to the High Horse Saloon and Eatery. High Horse Saloon is a fun bar, but our favorite thing about it is the dancing. Every Tuesday at 7 p.m., the saloon hosts dance lessons followed by music and dancing until 10 p.m.—a great way to practice all those cool moves you just learned! A variety of dance styles are taught, from salsa to swing, but our favorite nights are the ones that focus on a Montana staple: country western dancing. Hungry Horse Saloon has dance class nights throughout the year that teach the Cowboy Jitterbug, the two-step, and the western cha cha. Once you've, no doubt, worked up an appetite from all the dancing, you're in the right place. The food at the High Horse Saloon and Eatery is excellent and it is consistently voted one of the best all-around restaurants in Billings.

3953 Montana Ave., 406-259-0111
thehighhorsesaloonandeatery.com/dance-lessons

ATTEND AN ANNUAL FUNDRAISER EVENT
FOR A GOOD CAUSE

The Billings community loves a reason to get together. Add in a good cause and it's even better. There are many events organized and participated in by locals that raise money for charity while also providing a sport, feast, or festival-type experience when doing so. The entertainment aspect makes these annual fundraisers a must-do event unto themselves. Here are some of the charity events we recommend attending:

Souper Bowl: Angela's Piazza (women's help center), February. Check their website for location. 406-255-0611, angelaspiazza.org

Relay for Life of Yellowstone Co.: The American Cancer Society, July. West High School Stadium, 2201 St. Johns Ave., 800-227-2345, secure.acsevents.org/site/STR?pg=entry&fr_id=105057

Brew Fest: PEAKS (People Everywhere Are Kind and Sharing) helping cancer patients and their families, July. ZooMontana, 2100 Shiloh Rd., 406-657-4670, peaksbillings.com

Burn the Point Parade and Car Show: Chase Hawks Memorial Association (grants to individuals and families in crisis), September. Downtown, 406-248-9295, chasehawks.com/events/burn-the-point

Ales for Trails: Billings TrailNet, September. ZooMontana, 2100 Shiloh Rd., 406-281-1244, alesfortrails.com

MORE CHARITY EVENTS

Rockin' under the Big Sky
Adult Resource Alliance, September

ZooMontana, 2100 Shiloh Rd., 406-259-9666
allianceyc.org

Whiskey and Wine
Billings Symphony, September

Henry's Garage, 12 Garden Ave., 406-855-7999
billingssymphony.org/shows/special-events/whiskey-wine-2

NILE Rodeo
Tough Enough to Wear Pink Night—EVA Project through St. Vincent Hospital Foundation, October

MetraPark Arena, 308 6th Ave. N, 406-237-3600
sclhealth.org/locations/st-vincent-healthcare-foundation/current-initiatives/eva-project

PRCA Roughstock Rodeo
Chase Hawks Memorial Foundation (grants to individuals and families in crisis), December

MetraPark Arena, 308 6th Ave. N, 406-248-9295
chasehawks.com/events/roughstock-weekend/roughstock-rodeo

Polar Plunge
Special Olympics Montana,
December, check website for location

800-242-6876
somt.org/events/billings-polar-plunge

RUN WITH THE SHEEP
IN REED POINT

Forget the running of the bulls. In Montana, we have the running of the sheep. And it happens every year in the town of Reed Point, 60 miles west of Billings. For over 30 years, the Great Montana Sheep Drive festival has been delighting attendees with fun, games, food, and camaraderie. The highlight is watching hundreds of sheep run down Main Street right through the middle of the festival. The sheep run typically happens in late afternoon, but there's a whole day's worth of entertainment before that. Wake up early and partake in the Fireman's Breakfast, enter the hay bale rolling and log sawing contests, stay for the evening street dance with live music, watch a small-town parade, bid for items at a charity auction, and feast on cuisine from food vendors. Families will appreciate the kiddie rides and petting zoo area.

Main Street, Reed Point
stillwatercountychamber.com/about/chamber-event-galleries/reed-point-sheep-drive

JAZZ UP YOUR LIFE
AT LEVITY BAR AND BISTRO

Sit back with a cocktail and enjoy the smooth sound of local jazz musicians as they jam on Wednesday nights from 7 p.m. to 9 p.m. at Levity Bar and Casino. The Wednesday night jazz session serves as an open mic of sorts. As you sit there listening to jazz and tapping your foot along to the music, enjoy some delicious pizza and cheese boards alongside an assortment of libations. Want to move more than just your foot? Dancing is perfectly acceptable and you'll often see several couples spinning around the floor in front of the band. Show up early to get a good seat; this is a popular weekly night out for those in the know so tables fill up quickly.

There are gaming machines in an adjoining room if you prefer jazz as your background music for a little gambling.

1027 Shiloh Crossing Blvd., Unit 8, 406-651-5985
facebook.com/levitybar

TIP

If you play a jazz instrument and would like to jam with the house band, you can often show up and play. Vocalists are welcomed, too; just ask first.

31

SHOW OFF YOUR RANDOM KNOWLEDGE

AT TRIVIA NIGHT

Take advantage of all those random facts taking up real estate in your brain every Tuesday night at the Vig Alehouse, a lively sports bar that hosts a popular trivia night each Tuesday. Trivia nights are hosted by DJ McLovin, a local radio celebrity in Billings who makes the evening fun and engaging while fostering some friendly competition. In between puzzling over the answers, you can enjoy some American pub fare like gourmet mac and cheese or a plate of brisket nachos. And of course there's a full bar; just make sure you don't get fuzzy about those facts! Winners get a small cash prize—you can tuck it into your wallet or continue the night of fun by putting it toward another round of beer or some of those other yummy choices on the menu.

501 Hilltop Rd., 406-281-8484
thevigalehouse.com

TIP

Want to try a trivia night with a pop culture theme? Manny's Sports Bar also does trivia on Tuesday nights. Follow their Facebook page to see what trivia themes are coming up. In the past, they've had Harry Potter, Pokemon, '90s Nickelodeon, and holiday-themed nights. If bingo is more your jam, Manny's also hosts bingo every Wednesday. 4241 Kari Ln., 406-655-7979, facebook.com/mannysbillings

SING YOUR HEART OUT
AT CRYSTAL LOUNGE

Stake your claim as the king or queen of karaoke at Crystal Lounge and Casino. If you love showing off your singing chops in front of a great crowd on a big karaoke stage, this is the place to go in Billings. Crystal Lounge has a fun, upbeat atmosphere where even newcomers are welcomed. Food and drinks are available so you can fill up or get some liquid courage before your name is called to perform. Crystal Lounge makes it easy to up your sing-along game with karaoke every night of the week. So grab your friends, pick up that microphone, and sing your heart out! Perhaps you'll duet it up with the karaoke staple "Summer Lovin'" or hit all the right notes on your own as you belt out a modern ballad or rock anthem. Whatever you choose, karaoke at Crystal Lounge is sure to be a hoot.

101 N Broadway, 406-259-0010
facebook.com/CrystalLoungeBillings

TIP

If you like to have some fun gambling, Crystal Lounge and Casino is one of the largest casinos in Billings. It has slot machines, blackjack tables, and poker tournaments with low buy-ins.

CHASE YOUR BLUES AWAY

AT THE MAGIC CITY BLUES FESTIVAL

Enjoy the good kind of blues at the annual Magic City Blues Festival in Billings. Playing more than just the blues, this festival parlays into country, alternative, and rock, and has become known as "Montana's Urban Music Festival." It takes place over two music-filled days in August. Held in Billings's prominent MetraPark Arena, concert attendees can be assured of high-quality sound and acoustics with enough space to dance the night away and plenty of food and drink options. Shows are typically happening on multiple outdoor stages during the festival so be sure to check the schedule throughout the event to make sure you don't miss your favorite artists. The lineup changes every year. In the past, the festival has played host to the likes of the Steve Miller Band, ZZ Top, Blues Traveler, Lynyrd Skynyrd, Alison Krauss, Ziggy Marley, and Counting Crows among many other world-class bands.

308 6th Ave. N, 406-534-0400
magiccityblues.com

BET ON THE PIG RACES
AT BEAR CREEK DOWNS

Forget horse racing. In Bearcreek each summer it's all about the pigs. Located just east of Red Lodge and an hour from Billings is Bear Creek Saloon and Steakhouse, which is where you'll find a bunch of little oinkers racing when the weather warms up. On Thursday through Sunday evenings in the summer, the outdoor area by the saloon is transformed into a racecourse with whoops and hollers as pigs are released from their chutes and (often distractedly) make their way around the track to the finish line. Bets are taken for which pig will be first, but the racing and betting is all in good fun. The pigs are well taken care of and proceeds from the event go to fund local schools. The pigs are so cute you might even find yourself staying away from the bacon afterward! Luckily, Bear Creek Saloon has a wide range of options on their menu for both food and drinks.

14 W Main St., Bearcreek, 406-446-3481
redlodge.com/bearcreek

FIND YOUR WAY THROUGH THE MAIZE

AT GRANDPA'S FARM

Fall fun awaits at this family-favorite farm festival. The Maize at Grandpa's Farm is the place to go when the weather gets crisp and Halloween is just around the corner. As the name suggests, this annual festival is home to a corn maze—and it's a massive one with incredible attention to detail. The maze changes each year with new theme designs. In addition to the maze, there are games, tractor-pull rides, a petting zoo, a pumpkin patch, slides built on and around a haystack, and so much more. Concession stands are also at Grandpa's Farm selling treats like hot chocolate, kettle corn, candy, and other yummy snacks. The Maize at Grandpa's Farm typically opens up in early to mid-September and is open through October 30. Fridays and Saturdays in October are when the haunted maze part of the farm is open for some spooky excitement to get you in the Halloween spirit!

2201 58th St. W, 406-696-6266
themaizeatgrandpasfarm.com

36

GET FRIGHTENED FOR CHARITY

AT SCARITY HAUNTED HOUSE

Spooky thrills await at this seriously scary haunted house that has popped up each fall since 2018 to raise money for a good cause. Scarity Haunted House has become a must-do for many people every October to get in the Halloween spirit while helping fund local charities. Upping the cool factor is a venue location perfect for scares: the historic Depot building in downtown Billings. Scarity Haunted House is made possible by many volunteers who help with design, makeup, costumes, ticket sales, and spooky acting to get some screams. Be aware that there are gory and frightful scenes that may be too scary for some kids and teens, or any age that can't handle scary stuff well! But if you find a big dose of fear to be part of the fun, then you'll love this haunted house.

2310 Montana Ave., 406-702-2011
facebook.com/scarityhauntedhouse

TIP

Scarity usually offers tamer nights for those five and up who don't want such big scares. "R-rated" extra scary nights are also offered. Check the schedule to see what level of scare factor is being performed nightly.

37

STOMP GRAPES
AT YELLOWSTONE CELLARS AND WINERY

Leave your shoes behind and get ready to stomp up a storm at the Yellowstone Cellars and Winery Annual Grape Stomp. Feel the juice ooze between your toes as you laugh and squish your way around the grapes. You'll even be contributing to the wine making process; the grapes being stomped on will actually be fermented and used in wines that will come out about two to three years after the event. Before the stomping begins, a pastor comes to bless the grapes. After the big grape stomp, there is live music and dancing with food and drinks available. The Yellowstone Cellars and Winery Grape Stomp takes place each September on the winery premises located right in Billings. When it's not the festival weekend, you'll still find wine tasting and live music most weekends in the winery's tasting room and adjacent patio.

1335 Holiday Circle, 406-281-8400
yellowstonecellars.com

TAKE A BOW
WITH COMMUNITY THEATER

Ready to see your name up in lights on the big stage? OK, maybe Hollywood's not calling yet, but if you have dreams of performing, the Billings Studio Theatre and NOVA Center for the Performing Arts are two great places to get your start. Billings Studio Theatre is a community-focused company that has been performing since 1956 and continues to innovate and grow with each passing year. Keep an eye out for upcoming casting calls for your chance to get your big break. Stagehands and production crew volunteer opportunities are also often available if you're more of a behind-the-scenes theater person. NOVA also has opportunities for working on your craft with regular theater classes and performances for both adults and youth. Improv more your flavor? Look into joining their resident improv troupe.

1500 Rimrock Rd., 406-248-1141
billingsstudiotheatre.com

2317 Montana Ave., 406-591-9535
novabillings.org

TIP

Another way to get involved in local theater is to volunteer in a non-acting role for the traveling troupe for Shakespeare in the Park when they come to Billings each year. 406-994-3310, shakespeareintheparks.org

Steepworld

SPORTS AND RECREATION

39

ENJOY CITY AND MOUNTAIN VISTAS
FROM ON TOP OF THE RIMS

No doubt the most spectacular and prettiest thing about Billings is the line of towering sandstone cliffs bordering the north and southeast sides of the city. They are known as the Rimrocks—or as the locals refer to them, simply "the Rims." Seeing the Rims from down below while driving around town is always lovely, but an even better experience is from up above, walking and exploring right along the top in one of the city parks: Zimmerman Park on the western end of the north rims and Swords Park on the east. Across the river you will have equally spectacular views from the Four Dances Recreation Area. The Rims are where people go for simple yet romantic sunset-viewing date nights, or a peaceful morning walk as you gaze at the entirety of Billings spread out below you. Depending on your viewing location, you can see five or more mountain ranges in the distance. On a clear day when there is snow in the mountains, you can even see the ski runs of Red Lodge Mountain, more than 60 miles away.

Zimmerman Park, 3314 MT-3
Swords Park, Swords Park Dr.
billingsparks.org/parks-trail, 406-657-8371

Four Dances Recreation Area, 1100 Coburn Rd.
blm.gov/visit/four-dances-srma, 406-896-5013

BIKE AND HIKE

An extensive trail system around the city of Billings will eventually create a full marathon loop of 26.2 miles. The current main trail sections are listed below.

- Swords Park Trail and the Chief Black Otter Trail; east end of the Rims
- Zimmerman Park Trail; west end of the Rims
- Skyline Trail; 10 feet wide, accessible for wheelchairs, connecting Swords Park to Zimmerman Park on the Rims
- Inner Belt Loop; connecting Hwy. 3 to the Heights
- Jim Dutcher Trail; east
- Riverfront Park Trail; south

There are also several trails within the city that provide biking, walking, and running enjoyment. To easily find locations of the city trails, download the Billings Heritage Trails app.

Find more information about Billings' trails, plans and progress on additional trails, plus fundraising activities at billingstrailnet.org.

E-bikes are a fun way to make exploring the city more accessible and are allowed on all the city trails. Rentals are available at these shops:

Pedego Electric Bikes Billings, 820 Shiloh Crossing Blvd.
406-248-1515
pedegoelectricbikes.com/dealers/billings

The Spoke Shop, 1910 Broadwater Ave., 406-656-8342
spokeshop.com

ACE A HOLE

PLAYING DISC GOLF ON THE RIMS AT DIAMOND X IN PHIPPS PARK

OK, we might be biased, but Billings has one of the coolest places to play disc golf in the country. At Phipps Park, you can try your hand at Frisbee throwing or show off your expertise by landing a hole in one at the Diamond X disc golf course, known as one of the most challenging and bucket-list–worthy courses in the sport. Oh, and did we mention it's located on top of the renowned Rimrocks? You'll be tossing that Frisbee disc while traversing the hilly trails of the Rims. While you're aiming your Frisbee toward the baskets, take breaks from the sport to take in gorgeous views of the Billings cityscape and distant mountain ranges. You'll have plenty of time to do so if you play all three courses, a total of 36 holes, which will also let you get in a good workout as you climb all over Phipps Park to play the courses.

6790 Molt Rd., 406-657-8371
discgolfbillings.com

TAKE YOURSELF OUT
TO A BALL GAME

Billings may not be home to any major-league sports teams, but you wouldn't know that on a night at Dehler Park when the Mustangs are playing. The Billings Mustangs are a minor-league baseball team, but they play a big game under the city lights at the 3,071-seat Dehler Park stadium. As the rookie affiliate of the Cincinnati Reds, the Mustangs take their baseball seriously, as do their loyal fans. Don't miss spotting the statue of Dave McNally in front of the stadium. McNally was a hometown boy who became a pitcher for the Baltimore Orioles and helped them win two World Series championships. The outdoor ambiance with the Rims in the background, concession stand staples, and the community bonding at each Mustangs game makes this a must-do activity during baseball season for families in Billings. If you've never experienced the fun of a Mustangs game at Dehler Park, then it's time to take yourself out to the ball game next season and embrace "America's national pastime."

2611 9th Ave. N, 406-252-1241
billingsmustangs.com

RIDE THE RAPIDS
OF THE STILLWATER RIVER

Experience the wild rapids of the Stillwater River as you dip and careen down fast-flowing rivers that dramatically curve through the western plains landscape. With rapid names like Mad Max, Beartooth Drop, and Sideswipe, your adrenaline will be coursing as quickly as the river as your raft hits each drop. Unless you're an extremely experienced whitewater rafter, it's best to do this activity with a guide. Check out Adventure Whitewater, based an hour west of Billings just outside of Absarokee. Adventure Whitewater has its own private launch on the Stillwater River. They offer half-day rafting trips as well as full-day "Paddle n' Saddle" excursions that combine whitewater rafting with horseback riding. The part of the river you'll be floating on will differ depending on the time of year and the level of rapids you want; Adventure Whitewater has been around for over 30 years and knows the river backward and forward. In late summer, they may even switch things up to the Yellowstone River, depending on water levels and conditions.

1 N Stillwater Rd., Absarokee, 800-897-3061
adventurewhitewater.com

REV UP
AT THE GREAT AMERICAN PRO CHAMPIONSHIP HILL CLIMB

Did you know the longest-running motorbike event in the country takes place in Billings each summer? For over a century, motorcyclists have been racing up the steep incline and tough terrain of the hills south of the Yellowstone River. This rugged landscape provides a climb so challenging for professionals that it has even been nicknamed "the hill climbing capital of the world." This is an epic event to watch since it's open only to pro bikers who come from around the world in an attempt to win the large championship purse. Run by the Billings Motorcycle Club, the two-day event hosts multiple competitions and race-offs. If you don't want to miss any of the action, your best bet is to book one of the tent or RV sites on the event grounds. Concessions are available on-site or it's a 1.5-mile walk to a market and gas station.

3630 Old Blue Creek Rd.
bmcmontana.com/events

TIP

Want to try nonmotorized dirt biking yourself? Visit the track at Blue Creek Bike Park, a pump track just 2.5 miles west of Billings Motorcycle Club. 1939 Blue Creek Rd., 406-647-0252, bluecreekbikepark.com

44

ROOT FOR THE COWBOY WAY OF LIFE

AT A RODEO

The first time you go to a rodeo, the noise and frenetic pace of the animals and riders with their gasp-inducing stunts can feel overwhelming. Soon, though, you'll settle into the fun and drama and theatrical display of cowboy culture in Montana. During the summer, there's a rodeo going on in or near Billings pretty much every weekend. Even in winter, rodeos keep going in enclosed arenas. When choosing a rodeo to attend, it's important to understand the difference between Professional Rodeo Cowboys Association (PRCA) and ranch rodeos. PRCA hosts a number of big rodeos around the area. You'll get to see exciting events like bull riding, barrel racing, and bareback riding. Ranch rodeos, on the other hand, do not feature professional rodeo performers; instead, it's usually teams of ranch hands who demonstrate working skills and compete, for the fun of it, to see who's best. The events can include team trailering, roping, branding, doctoring, milking a wild cow—and sometimes individual bronc riding.

TIP

If attending a rodeo at MetraPark, take time to view the Montana Pro Rodeo's Wall of Fame located in the complex.

Professional Bull Riders (PBR) Rodeo
This rodeo featuring only the bull riding events is held mid-April at MetraPark Arena.

308 6th Ave. N, 719-242-2800, pbr.com

Red Lodge Home of Champions Rodeo
Red Lodge is the place to be for your Fourth of July holiday. Enjoy three days of rodeos, parades, and western fun.

101 Rodeo Dr., Red Lodge, 406-446-2422, redlodgerodeo.com

Big Timber Weekly Pro Rodeo
Weekly rodeo on Wednesday evenings for six consecutive weeks beginning in August.

78 Fairgrounds Rd., Big Timber, 406-930-2885, jsrodeocompany.com

MontanaFair Rodeo
The PRCA Rodeo during MontanaFair typically occurs for three nights at the end of fair week in mid-August at MetraPark Arena.

308 6th Ave. N, 406-256-2400, montanafair.com

NILE Rodeo
Three nights of PRCA rodeos with top-ranking competitors and a ranch rodeo in which ranch cowboys put their working skills to the test. Mid-October at MetraPark Arena.

308 6th Ave. N, 406-256-2400, thenile.org

Chase Hawks Roughstock PRCA Rodeo
Roughstock rodeos consist of three events: bareback riding, saddle bronc riding, and bull riding. Mid-December at MetraPark Arena.

308 6th Ave. N, 406-256-2400, chasehawks.com

Miller's Horse Palace
Year-round events. Watch cowboys and cowgirls of all ages practice and compete in barrel racing and roping events. The Little Britches Rodeos are great fun to watch as kids as young as five compete in events by age group.

7215 Mossman Ln., 406-628-4100, millershorsepalace.org

GLIDE THROUGH THE SNOW
AT RED LODGE

Downhill, cross-country, and terrain parks . . . Red Lodge ski areas have it all. So grab your favorite pair of skis or snowboard and head west to this popular mountain location that's a local winter playground for southeastern Montanans. From Billings, it's approximately one hour to the ski area. You'll drive through the little historic downtown area of Red Lodge where you'll no doubt see some places you might want to go for an après drink or meal. For downhill skiers and boarders, Red Lodge Mountain has 70 runs across 1,635 acres ranging from beginner to expert level. If cross-country skiing is more your jam, the Red Lodge Nordic Center at Aspen Ridge Ranch has the best groomed trails in the region, offering both classic skiing tracks and a skate skiing lane.

Red Lodge Mountain
305 Ski Run Rd., 406-446-2610
redlodgemountain.com

Red Lodge Nordic Center at Aspen Ridge Ranch
beartoothtrails.org/winter-trails

In March, visit Red Lodge during the National Finals Skijoring Races—western style, meaning skiers are pulled behind a horse and rider. The race involves skiing through a course of gates and jumps for the fastest time.

redlodgeskijoring.com

SPEND AN AFTERNOON PADDLING
ON LAKE ELMO

Lake Elmo is a 64-acre reservoir within the 123-acre Lake Elmo State Park. This picturesque park on the northeast side of Billings makes the trendy sport of paddleboarding easy to try. The water is typically calm, making it a great place to get your balance on the board or get in a good workout. Effortlessly launch your board from the beach and then take off across the lake, leaving the swimmers behind for some pretty scenery and solitude. Paddling a canoe or kayak are also options if you want more stability. Bird-watching is a fun activity to do as you navigate your watercraft around the lake. Lake Elmo State Park has a playground, a dog park, a fishing dock, and a 1.4-mile nature trail that circles the lake. For nature lovers looking for an easy way to spend some time outdoors in Billings, it's a truly great spot.

219 Rolling Hills Dr., 406-247-2940
fwp.mt.gov/stateparks/lake-elmo

TIP

If you don't have your own stand-up paddleboard, canoe, or kayak, there are a few places to rent them around Billings. We recommend SunShine Sports. They have a great, reasonably priced paddlesports rental program with stand-up paddleboards, canoes, kayaks, and accessories. Base Camp (page 114) and Scheels (page 115) also have rental options.

304 Moore Ln., 406-252-3724
sunshine-sports.com

DRIVE
THE SWITCHBACKS OF THE BEARTOOTH HIGHWAY

The Beartooth Highway is listed on many "best of" lists as one of the most beautiful drives in America. It has a wildly steep and twisting climb to an altitude of 10,964 feet. Along with vistas of mountain peaks and deep canyons, this picturesque drive takes you through alpine tundra and a high plateau with panoramic views of clear lakes, wildflowers, and snowfields. Watch for the sign that directs your eye to the "Bear's Tooth" rock spire in the distance, and look for mountain goats in the meadows. A doable day trip from Billings, the Beartooth Highway starts in Red Lodge and ends in Cooke City by the northeast entrance to Yellowstone National Park. The Beartooth Highway is typically open from Memorial Day weekend to mid-September, depending on snowfall and plow removal.

mdt.mt.gov/travinfo/beartooth

Watch for die-hard adventurers skiing in midsummer at the Beartooth Basin Summer Ski Area located at the top of the drive. There are two platter-style chairlifts and nine runs along the Twin Lakes Headwall. Skiing here is not recommended for beginners though; the runs are all advanced intermediate or expert level.

HUNT FOR MONTANA MOSS AGATES
ALONG THE YELLOWSTONE RIVER

Who didn't pick up rocks as a kid?! Remind yourself of that fun childhood pastime while in Billings with an amble along the Yellowstone River Basin. This area is a rock hound's playground and the only place to find Montana moss agates. What makes this type of agate coveted is the translucent interior with imbedded dark spots of moss and dendrites creating a beautiful scene that is revealed when the rock is sliced open. Hunting for them is an easy activity to do, though it takes some practice knowing what to look for. Telltale signs are a coating (usually shiny white, but it can be dull yellow-white or even black) with divots or hairline fractures on the surface. Moss agates are pretty in their natural state but to see the beauty that awaits inside, take them to a rock cutter or invest in a rock saw.

TIP

Don't want to do the hunting, but want the agate? Check out Stones and Bones, a lapidary jewelry and loose rock store that has just about every stone you can imagine, including agate rocks, slices, decorative accessories, and jewelry (even agate marbles!). 701 24th St. W, #1, 406-671-4160 facebook.com/StonesandBonesBillings

GIDDYUP
AT BITTER CREEK OUTFITTERS

Is there anything more quintessentially Montana than riding a horse through the hills? While it's not true that everyone in Montana has a horse, you can't deny the romance and history that is evoked with horseback riding. There is something magical about exploring the natural world on the back of a gentle beast. If you're not a skilled rider and don't have your own horse, you can still easily achieve this experience near Billings thanks to Bitter Creek Outfitters. This woman-owned (make that cowgirl-owned!) company offers trail rides for all experience levels right outside Billings on a 7,000-acre working cattle ranch. Small group tours are expertly led by skilled horse wranglers on expertly picked trails that go along the top of the Rimrocks for incredible views. You'll feel secure as you explore valley and riverside scenery. Most tours include a stop for a refreshment and snack break.

2405 Coburn Rd., 406-855-6075
bittercreekoutfitters.com

50

CAST A LINE ON THE YELLOWSTONE TO CATCH A BIG ONE

There's nothing quite like the thrill of getting your cast just right so the winged insect at the end of your fishing rod seemingly skips across the surface of the water. It takes a lot of practice to perfect fly fishing, but Billings is a great place to begin thanks to its close proximity to the Yellowstone River. If you're new to the sport, your best bet is to go with a fishing outfitter in Billings that can set you up with the proper gear, take you to good spots for beginners, and teach you helpful techniques. Want to learn the basics first? Take the "Learn to Fly Fish" course that is offered each year through Billings Parks and Recreation.

Guides: Montana Adventures and Angling
406-855-3612, mtangling.com
(We've used Nate Plagmann, Montana on the Fly.
He was a great guide and we caught a lot of fish!)

Where to Get Gear: East Rosebud Tackle Shop
960 S 24th St. W, Ste. A, 406-839-9397
eastrosebudflyandtackle.com

Fly Fishing Course: billingsparks.org/program/learn-to-fly-fish

TIP
If you're "hooked" and ready for some blue-ribbon fishing, drive an hour to the Bighorn River public access sites near Fort Smith. This area is considered one of the best trout fishing spots in the US!

SPEND THE NIGHT
AT AMERICA'S FIRST KOA CAMPGROUND

Most of us have heard of KOA campgrounds. But did you know the very first KOA campground was built and is still operating in Billings? That was in 1967. KOA is now a multimillion-dollar company with hundreds of campgrounds across the US, and the headquarters are still here in Billings. The Billings KOA Holiday has been run by a local family since the 1970s and is an award-winning campground. It aims to foster community and bring new friends together around a campfire. In recent years, there's also been a big focus on ensuring modern comforts like Internet access, sports and rec areas, clean bathrooms, and an on-site grocery store and café. More fun is created with ice cream socials, an adventure golf course, and a heated swimming pool. Tent and RV sites with hookups are available. Billings KOA Holiday is open from April 1 through October 31.

547 Garden Ave., 406-252-3104
koa.com/campgrounds/billings

TIP

If tents and RVs aren't your thing, you can book one of the campground's log cabins, which can sleep up to six people. Each cabin has a kitchen and bathroom plus a relaxing little patio. Budget-friendly camping cabins are also available to rent, which don't have bathrooms or kitchens and require you to bring your own linens.

MAKE A SPLASH INDOORS AND OUT

AT BILLINGS WATER PARKS

Billings is lucky to have not just one but two fun water parks. Splish and splash and race down waterslides year-round since Oasis is outdoors and the Reef Water Park is indoors. Let's talk about Oasis first. This is the place to go for water-loving families during the summer from June to August. It has a play structure in the water, multiple pools, a lagoon, and two-story-tall slides. In summer, this is our top pick. When the weather gets frigid, you can head to the Reef Indoor Water Park for some more water fun. It's a kiddie paradise with a wave pool and huge water playground. Two massive tube slides wind down from above, while young children will enjoy the shorter playground slides. The Reef is part of the Bighorn Resort but has day passes available for those not staying at the hotel.

Oasis Water Park
543 Aronson Ave., 406-969-3131
billingsoasis.com

The Reef Indoor Water Park
1801 Majestic Ln., 406-839-9283
thereefindocrs.com

53

EXPLORE THE YELLOWSTONE RIVER ECOSYSTEM

AT THE RIVERFRONT PARK COMPLEX

Riverfront Park is on the edge of the Billings city limits, but as soon as you begin walking along its trails, you'll feel like you're many miles away from urban dwellings. A series of loop trails take you around peaceful lakes and alongside the Yellowstone River. Pause for a rest and snack at one of the numerous picnic tables located all around Riverfront Park. Birds are nearly always seen and sometimes seem to take over the park in warmer months. To really get in touch with the local wildlife and bird-watching, head west across South Billings Boulevard to the Norm Schoenthal Island part of the Riverfront Park complex. "Norm's Island" is a unique island that is located right in the middle of the river but is accessible via a couple of bridges—when not covered in water. The entire island is flooded for a short time every year during late spring, but this yearly transformation aids in its diverse ecology.

8001 S Billings Blvd., 406-657-8371
billingsparks.org/location/riverfront

54

BOAT
THROUGH BIGHORN CANYON NATIONAL RECREATION AREA

Bighorn Canyon National Recreation Area is a remote, hidden gem of a destination in Montana that is blissfully devoid of crowds. What else makes Bighorn Canyon so special? Deep blue water flowing through a red-tinged canyon created by the Yellowtail Dam. Bighorn Canyon has been called the little Grand Canyon due to its impressively high and steep cliffs surrounding the calm water. The water of Bighorn Lake is cold even at the height of summer, though not so cold that you can't swim in it. Bighorn Canyon is definitely a doable day trip from Billings and takes about two hours to drive. Once you get there you'll find a parking lot right by the boat launch. No boat? No problem. Ok-A-Beh Marina has pontoons for rent. Plan ahead and make your reservation online.

Bighorn Canyon National Recreation Area, Fort Smith
Ok-A-Beh Marina Boat Rentals: 406-384-6930
nps.gov/bica/index.htm

TIP

Be sure to bring sun protection and a map—there is no shade or cell service. Also, it's a good idea to fill up with gas in Hardin and get snacks and water if needed since there's not much between Hardin and the marina.

CHEER ON MONTANA ATHLETES
AT THE BIG SKY STATE GAMES

The Big Sky State Games, hosted every summer in Billings, are a big deal. They may not be the actual Olympics, but they follow a similar format and even have a torch lighting ceremony. The Big Sky State Games are recognized by the US Olympic Committee and are open to the public to watch. Montana joined the state games in 1986 and it has rapidly grown since then with the highest per capita participation of all 30 state games in the nation. Over 10,000 amateur participants now compete in 35 different sports coming from 250 different communities in Montana. It has launched sport careers, showcased future and former Olympians, and helped cultivate a sense of pride for the sporting communities in Montana. Proceeds from the event go toward many initiatives for health and sports, including Big Sky Fit Kids and Shape Up Montana.

Daylis Stadium, 401 Grand Ave., 406-254-7426
bigskygames.org

START YOUR ENGINES
AND HEAD TO THE YELLOWSTONE DRAG STRIP

Marvel at the speed of a drag race at this track that is considered a hidden gem in the racing community. Cheer on the drivers as they showcase their souped-up cars and take them on exciting races around the track. In addition to drag racing, the track hosts other vehicle-themed events throughout the year, such as the Big Sky Truck Fest or an all-Harley motorcycle race. For those who hope to be a future dragster star, check out the clinics the Yellowstone Drag Strip offers for junior racers. The Facebook page is the best way to keep up to date on future events. Yellowstone Drag Strip is sanctioned by the NHRA (National Hot Rod Association), locally owned and operated, and located in Acton, just 20 miles north of downtown Billings.

8405 Raceway Ln., Acton
yellowstonedragstrip.com

57

STARGAZE
AT ACTON RECREATION AREA

Montana is one of the darkest states of the lower 48, offering plenty of spectacular celestial night viewing. Billings is a small city surrounded by plains so the light pollution is still low, which means on a clear night, you can step outside and do some stargazing pretty much immediately. However, you may want to head to the top of the Rims or to a nearby park to really feel like you're in nature. To escape all traces of city lights and immerse yourself in the world of stargazing, head north to Acton Recreation Area. Look beyond the tall tips of the ponderosa pine trees for the explosion of stars shining bright above you, less than 30 miles from Billings. Acton Recreation Area is on Montana's Trail to the Stars, a site that has tips and links to apps and other information to aid in your night sky viewing experience.

Acton Recreation Area: Heag Rd., Acton
blm.gov/visit/acton
trailtothestars.com

"CLIMB ON" AT STEEPWORLD

Rock climbing is a popular pastime in Montana. Getting into the gravity-defying activity of rock climbing can feel a bit daunting though. Luckily there's an easy way to get your footing for the sport in Billings: Steepworld Climbing and Fitness, a welcoming and community-focused indoor rock climbing gym that will have you climbing with ease in no time. It is family-friendly and has levels for everyone—even toddlers can be seen climbing up sections of wall. Most of the climbing wall has auto belays while routes in the lead and top rope areas require a climbing partner. The tallest route is 42 feet high. Steepworld's friendly staff will literally show you the ropes—helping you get acquainted with harnesses, climbing shoes, chalk, and best practices for safety. Climbing technique classes are available upon request for groups or individuals. Top rope and lead climbing classes and certification are also offered for those wanting to take their skills to the next level.

1230 S 31st St. W. 406-969-2500
steepworld.com

TIP

There are bouldering sections on the main and upper levels, which provide great practice for beginners and anyone wanting to work on their grip, foot placement, and climbing-without-gear skills.

Western Heritage Center

CULTURE AND HISTORY

TAKE A WALKING TOUR OF HISTORICAL SITES

ARRANGED BY THE WESTERN HERITAGE CENTER

Billings has a vast and varied history, and one of the best places to learn about the city's past is at the Western Heritage Center. As its name suggests, this local museum is focused on the history of the western plains and culture. Its exhibits are mostly about Montana, especially the people and places around the Yellowstone River Valley and the Northern High Plains. The Western Heritage Center features this history through both permanent and temporary exhibits. The permanent collection features over 35,000 pieces of art and memorabilia. As you walk through the center you'll be able to view old photographs and architectural drawings, Native American art and beadwork, western wear and other styles of decades past, oral histories, and so much more.

2822 Montana Ave., 406-256-6809
ywhc.org

TIP

One of the best ways to learn about the history of Billings is on one of the Western Heritage Center's guided walking tours through downtown Billings. Also, from the comfort of your home, listen to a speaker with the "High Noon Lecture Series." ywhc.org/museum-programs/historic-walking-tours, ywhc.org/museum-programs/lecture-series

COUNTY MUSEUMS FOR HISTORY BUFFS

Yellowstone County Museum

Informative displays of early ranching life and of early Native American culture, tools, and regalia are the focus of this museum.

1950 Terminal Circle, 406-256-6811, ycmhistory.org

Huntley Project Museum

A large photo gallery provides a historical look at the installation of the irrigation systems and agriculture of the Yellowstone River valley. Original buildings of the valley have been relocated and furnished to depict early-day farming life.

770 Railroad Hwy., Huntley, 406-348-2533, huntleyprojectmuseum.com

Treasure County '89ers Museum and Yucca Theatre

In addition to antiques and memorabilia from pioneer days in the area, you will find a fascinating collection of space exploration items donated by local resident Frank Borman, a NASA astronaut who flew with the Apollo 8 mission around the moon in 1968. Across the street is the restored Yucca Theatre.

325 Elliott Ave., Hysham, 406-342-5252

Big Horn County Historical Museum

The largest museum in the area, it is home to 24 carefully preserved historic structures, filled with exhibits. Antique equipment from the horse-drawn to the motorized are displayed inside large buildings. The history and culture of the Plains Indians of the area are displayed inside the main building.

1163 3rd St. E, Hardin, 406-665-1671, bighorncountymuseum.org

Carbon County Historical Society and Museum

A large collection of rodeo memorabilia from two rodeo families and other western artifacts are on display. There is also an immersive exhibit of mining that has a long history in the area.

224 Broadway Ave. N, Red Lodge, 406-446-3667, carboncountyhistory.com

Museum of the Beartooths

From covered wagons to railroad exhibits and a large display of the Apsáalooke culture, this small museum is well curated to give an informative look at early life in Stillwater County.

440 E 5th Ave. N, Columbus, 406-322-4588, museumofthebeartooths.com

IMAGINE WEALTHY LIVING IN THE EARLY 20TH CENTURY

AT THE MOSS MANSION

Stately homes that belonged to the nouveau riche of the early 20th century aren't just in the historic neighborhoods of New England. We have a mansion right here in downtown Billings that will make you feel like you've stepped back in time. The Moss Mansion was built in 1903 by a wealthy entrepreneur, Preston Boyd (P.B.) Moss and his wife, Mattie, who moved to Billings in 1892. The mansion was designed by Henry Janeway Hardenbergh, an architect who also designed the original Waldorf-Astoria Hotel and Park Hotel. P.B. and Mattie's middle child, Melville, lived in the house until she passed away in 1984. She is credited with preserving much of the original aesthetic of the mansion. Today, Moss Mansion is open to the public for tours and is listed on the National Register of Historic Places. Visiting it is a great way to see architecture and furnishings from the era. You'll also learn more about Billings's past and those who helped mold the city.

914 Division St., 406-256-5100
mossmansion.com

TIP

Moss Mansion is gorgeously decorated for the holidays with Christmas lights and trees. It's a fun, festive time to tour the mansion. Other seasonal events include Springfest with vendors and live music and a haunted maze at Halloween. The Murder Mystery Dinners held at Moss Mansion are also an unforgettable night out and tend to sell out quickly. Many more special tours and events are held throughout the year at Moss Mansion so always keep a close eye on their events page!

mossmansion.com/events

61

EXPERIENCE THE CULTURE OF THE SOUTH SIDE

AT THE MEXICAN FIESTA AND CAR SHOW

The Mexican Fiesta and Car Show at South Park is a chance for locals to celebrate their culture and heritage and share it with the Billings community. The family-friendly fiesta has run for almost 70 years and is held every summer. The Mexican Fiesta and Car Show features traditional dancing, music, food, and cars. The car show features a line of hot rods, sport coupes, and other cool vehicles being shown off by their proud owners. Select some delicious Mexican cuisine from one of the vendor stands and then watch the live music performances and dancers in their traditional costumes. This event is about friendship, family, and celebration of culture, but it's also for a good cause: the festival raises money to support the South Side neighborhood church, Mary Queen of Peace Catholic Church.

6th Ave. S and S 30th St., 406-259-7611
facebook.com/maryqueenofpeacebillings/events

The fun continues in the evening at the Mexican Fiesta Dance, typically held at the Billings Convention Center. Tickets are required for this part of the event and reserving a table is recommended.

facebook.com/BillingsMexicanFiestaDance

SEE CAVE DRAWINGS
BY SOME OF THE AREA'S EARLIEST INHABITANTS

Pictograph State Park is an alluring place of history and art located only 15 minutes from downtown Billings. This state park is small at just 23 acres, but still quite impressive due to a series of caves that are home to ancient drawings, called pictographs, some of which are believed to be at least 2,000 years old. These drawings can be seen on the walls of the park's largest cave, aptly called Pictograph Cave, and offer a glimpse into the life of indigenous tribes who hunted in the area. A three-quarter-mile loop trail connects three different caves, including Pictograph Cave, with interpretive signs along the length of the trail. While the cave drawings are the main feature of Pictograph State Park, don't miss a walk through the visitor center, which has more information about the indigenous tribes and over 30,000 artifacts excavated from the caves, including stone tools and weapons.

3401 Coburn Rd., 406-254-7342
fwp.mt.gov/stateparks/pictograph-cave

TIP

Bring binoculars to better see some of the drawings since the trail doesn't go all the way into the cave. In addition, consider visiting after a rainstorm or snowmelt as extra moisture in the cave tends to make the colors of the drawings more vibrant.

GLIMPSE WILD MUSTANGS RUNNING FREE IN THE PRYOR MOUNTAINS

Take a drive to the Pryor Mountains and view herds of wild mustangs running magnificently free, just 90 miles south of Billings. The Pryor Mountains Wild Horse Range is run by the Bureau of Land Management and is one of only four dedicated wild horse and burro ranges in the country. On your outing to see the wild horses, first stop at the Pryor Mountains Wild Mustang Center in Lowell, Wyoming, right over the border from Montana. At the center you can learn about the horses' Spanish and Portuguese ancestors and the history and behavior of the herd. The staff is very helpful and keeps track of the herd on a daily basis so they will be able to direct you to the best viewing areas. One of the easiest ways to see them is to book a tour with PryorWild Tours, a husband-and-wife team who work closely with the Mustang Center.

pryormustangs.org

DISCUSS ART WITH FRIENDS OLD AND NEW

AT ARTWALK

Celebrate art, people, and conversation in one place at ArtWalk. Every other month for four decades, the Downtown Billings Alliance has put on an ArtWalk on the first Friday of the month. It's a neat way to get the community together for music, food, drinks, and of course art. There is no cost to attend and walk through the galleries. Complimentary drinks and snacks are available at several of the venues. Each ArtWalk evening is a bit different, depending on the season, the art on display, and the vendors and musicians who may be participating. Often, local artists are featured and sometimes are even on-site to do talks during the event. A link to the map for each ArtWalk with participating businesses listed is usually posted on social media and the ArtWalk website the week before the event.

Downtown Billings, 406-690-1662
artwalkbillings.com

OTHER ART GALLERIES

Big Horn Design and Art Gallery

520 Wicks Ln., Ste. #6, 406-245-7327
bighornart.com

FarWest Gallery

2817 Montana Ave., 406-245-2334
farwestgallery.com

Montana Gallery

2710 2nd Ave. N, 406-672-9605
montanagallery.net

Sandstone Gallery

2913 2nd Ave. N, 406-256-5837
sandstonegallerymt.com

Sunrise Studio and Art Gallery

2923 Montana Ave., 406-294-0199
facebook.com/people/Sunrise-Studio-and-Gallery/100040057190952

Carbon County Arts Guild and Depot Gallery

11 8th St. W, Red Lodge, 406-446-1370
carboncountydepotgallery.org

Kinzley Photography Gallery and Studio

22 N Broadway Ave., Red Lodge, 406-445-3014
kinzleyphotography.com

MARVEL AT MODERN ART
WITH A VISIT TO THE YAM

This is the place to go in Billings to see modern art. Paintings, photography, sculptures, pottery, drawings, and more are on display at the Yellowstone Art Museum, commonly referred to as simply the YAM. The permanent collections at the YAM mostly highlight art by those who live or work within the regions of the Northern Plains and Northern Rocky Mountains. A carousel of new temporary exhibits occur throughout the year, often featuring Montana artists. If you fall in love with a particular artist or style of art, check if any pieces will be available at the annual art auction, held each winter. Feeling a bit artistic yourself? The YAM has art education programs for both children and adults. A variety of art technique classes are available as well as cooking and weekly yoga classes.

401 N 27th St., 406-256-6804
artmuseum.org

TIP

You won't want to miss SummerFair sponsored by the Yellowstone Art Museum. It's the largest arts and crafts fair in the region and is an excellent shopping opportunity. It's been running for over 45 years and now has more than 100 artists, community groups, and food vendors participating. Walk around the many booths to see what catches your eye, whether it's a new piece of artwork or a tantalizingly tasty treat.
artmuseum.org/engage/summerfair

ABSORB THE HISTORICAL IMPACT
OF THE BATTLE OF THE LITTLE BIGHORN

The Little Bighorn Battlefield National Monument is a memorial to the warriors of the Lakota Sioux, Northern Cheyenne, and Arapaho tribes, as well as the US soldiers of the 7th Cavalry who died here during the 1876 battle. It was a victory for the indigenous tribes, led by Chief Sitting Bull and Crazy Horse. The battle resulted in the deaths of the entire cavalry, led by Lt. Col. George A. Custer. The Little Bighorn Battlefield is a somber place to visit, but important to see and remember what the original inhabitants of the western plains had to do to fight for their way of life and land during the Plains Indian Wars. Little Bighorn Battlefield has informational boards located around the site to teach visitors about the battle. To learn even more, stop in the visitor center just down the road from the monument. Little Bighorn Battlefield National Monument isn't located in Billings, but it's well worth the drive to see.

I-90 Frontage Rd., Crow Agency, 406-638-2621
nps.gov/libi

TIP

Reenactment of the Battle of the Little Bighorn occurs at the end of June each year on a weekend close to its June 25 anniversary. Tickets are needed for the 90-minute event, which depicts the Battle of the Little Bighorn with live actors. littlebighornreenactment.com

67

EXPERIENCE WORLD-CLASS ART AND CONCERTS

UNDER THE BIG SKY

Husband-and-wife art enthusiasts and philanthropists Peter and Cathy Halstead provided a generous gift to the public when they selected the rolling Beartooth Mountain foothills for their vision of a sculpture and classical music setting in nature. Tippet Rise sits on 12,500 acres of a working ranch with large-scale sculptures standing alone in the vast landscape, most not visible one from another. Options for touring the sculptures are by bike, hike, or guided tour van. At each sculpture, you are able to walk up for a closer view of the design. The classical music concerts and recitals feature top musicians from all over the world; tickets are allotted each spring by a randomized drawing from entries submitted online. Occasionally there may be open concerts playing while you visit, but even if not, take time to enter the unique performance spaces, each designed to maximize the acoustical experience.

96 S Grove Creek Rd., Fishtail, 406-328-7820,
tippetrise.org

The entrance fee of $10 and reservation date and time need to be made in advance on their website. Lunch and dinner small-plate options along with wine from Prerogative Kitchen in Red Lodge are available in Will's Shed on-site.

CELEBRATE INDIGENOUS CULTURE
AT A POWWOW

Experiencing a powwow is an unforgettable life event. The powerful beating of drums, colorful regalia, and passionate dancing combine into a mesmerizing homage to ancestors and tradition. One of the best powwow events to attend is the annual Crow Fair, which is the largest Native American powwow in Montana and one of the largest in the entire country. It attracts more than 50,000 attendees every year and is open to everyone. Crow Fair has been going on for over a century and is held each summer on the grounds of the Crow Reservation, roughly an hour's drive from Billings. While attending, you'll be able to see traditional dancing and regalia, parades, Indian relay racing and other rodeo events, and traditional food like fry bread. It's also the largest gathering of teepees in the US. More than 1,000 are set up during the five-day festival for sleeping, giving the fair the nickname "Teepee Capital of the World."

Crow Agency, South of Hardin, 406-638-1447
www.crow-nsn.gov

TIP

If you're looking for a way to learn about Native American culture right in Billings, then check out the annual MSU-B Powwow held each spring on the campus of MSU Billings. 406-657-2182, msubillings.edu/naac/powwow.htm

LEARN ABOUT THE LAST CROW INDIAN CHIEF
AT CHIEF PLENTY COUPS STATE PARK

This special state park is named after one of the greatest diplomats in Montana history: Chief Plenty Coups, the last chief of the Crow Indian tribe. When the white man came, Chief Plenty Coups had a vision of the bison disappearing from the land. He concluded that the only way his people would survive was to work with instead of against the white man. He helped the US government fight against the Sioux and Cheyenne, who were the Crow's traditional enemies. He then negotiated for Crow reservation land in Montana. He built his own homestead on this land and learned to farm. He taught his people how to blend two worlds while always being an advocate for them and the reservation. Upon his death, he willed his land to the state to be a memorial and museum. While visiting, you'll learn about his life and history of the Crow tribe. You'll also see his original log home, the general store he ran, and sacred Medicine Spring.

1 Edgar/Pryor Road, Pryor, 406-252-1289
fwp.mt.gov/stateparks/chief-plenty-coups

ENCOURAGE YOUR CHILD'S LOVE OF SCIENCE AND INGENUITY

AT WISE WONDERS

Children will enjoy exploring the exhibits at Wise Wonders Science and Discovery Museum. This is one of the best places in Billings for families to spend an educational and engaging day learning about how things in our world work. Wise Wonders Discovery Museum is especially focused on STEM concepts, which it promotes through hands-on activities and interactive exhibits. Kids won't even realize they're learning science and problem-solving skills because the exhibits are so entertaining. An especially popular station is the grocery store where children can shop for grocery items, fill their cart, and learn about the checkout process in a fun child-centered setting. Making the experience even better is the low admission cost and a rotating schedule of special classes and activities, including robotics, art, building blocks, science experiments, and story time.

3024 2nd Ave. N, 406-702-1280
wisewonders.org

SEE A MOMENT IN TIME
AT POMPEYS PILLAR

Recapture the awe you felt learning about the Lewis and Clark Expedition during history class with a visit to Pompeys Pillar. This massive rock formation is made from sandstone and impressively juts up 120 feet close to the Yellowstone River. But what does this giant rock pillar have to do with Lewis and Clark? In 1806 the famous expedition came through this part of the Louisiana Purchase. When they arrived at what is now known as Pompeys Pillar, William Clark carved his name into the side of the sandstone. It's the only known signature made by either Lewis or Clark while on the expedition. To take a good look at the signature you'll have to climb several flights of stairs, but it's worth the exercise to see a preserved moment in history. Back down at ground level, don't leave Pompeys Pillar without touring the visitor center. It's packed with information, including exhibits about Sacajawea and indigenous life during that time period, as well as hardships the crew encountered during the exploration.

3039 Hwy. 312, 406-896-5013
pompeyspillar.org

BE A PIONEER FARMER FOR A DAY

AT THE THRESHING BEE

Antique tractors, in action, await you on the grounds of the Huntley Project Museum (which focuses on irrigated agriculture of the area) the third weekend of August at the Threshing Bee. What's threshing? It's the part of grain farming when the edible part of the grain is removed from the rest of the plant. The machinery that has done this over the past decades is on display during the Threshing Bee. A lot of this machinery, of horse, steam, and gas operation, still works and demonstrations are done throughout the festival. A sawmill and blacksmith shop can also be observed during the event. It's a family-friendly event that has food, farm-themed kiddie rides, and live music. All are welcomed to this annual celebration. Come learn about farming practices and history, while immersing yourself in the charm of a small-town festival less than 20 minutes from Billings.

770 Railroad Hwy.
antiquetractorclub.com

WATCH THE BIDDING ON LIVESTOCK

AT THE LOCAL AUCTION YARDS

Auctions are regularly held at the Billings Livestock Commission (BLS) and the Public Auction Yards (PAYS) right here in Billings. Watch the bidding to appreciate a key component of the ranching business in Montana. Or of course, if you're in the market for cattle, sheep, goats, or horses, feel free to make a bid! Horses and cattle are sold through the Billings Livestock Commission and cattle, sheep, and goats are sold through PAYS. Attending one of these auctions feels like something out of a movie, watching the livestock auctioned off as those around you bid for the best bloodlines and stock. Check the calendar on the BLS and PAYS websites for updates on auction times and dates.

Billings Livestock Commission
2443 N Frontage Rd., 406-245-4151, billingslivestock.com/horse-sales

Public Auction Yards
1802 Minnesota Ave., 406-245-6447, publicauctionyards.com

TIP

For the ultimate livestock auction, drive east to the small town of Miles City and attend the World Famous Miles City Bucking Horse Sale, held every May. In addition to the auctions, there are concerts, horse races, rodeo performances, street dances, and more at this annual event. buckinghorsesale.com

CREATE YOUR OWN ART
AT CROOKED LINE STUDIO

Crooked Line Studio is the place to go in Billings if you're looking to enhance your life through art creation. The studio offers a variety of classes for all types of art mediums. Every level of artist can find a class that suits them, and beginners are warmly welcomed. Workshop classes include projects like watercolor and oil paints, mixed media, cartooning, and sketching. Even pet portrait classes are occasionally offered! After-school art classes for kids are also available. Have your own vision? Embrace your inner artist at one of the open art nights where, for a small fee, you can show up with your project idea and work on whatever you want while coffee, Wi-Fi, and even some art supplies are provided. For those wanting to work on art at home, the knowledgeable staff can get you set up with all the tools you'll need from their retail section.

1206 24th St. W, 406-927-8041
crookedlinestudio.com

MORE PLACES TO CREATE ART

AR Workshop
Farmhouse and industrial DIY projects and classes

1595 Grand Ave., 406-630-2033
arworkshop.com/billings

Better to Gather
Classes on making stylish accessories for your home

208 N 13th St., 406-647-0835
bettertogather.com/classes

Bitterroot Sip and Paint
Private classes, open studio, and children's classes

1238 Central Ave., 406-318-9681
bitterrootsipandpaint.com

Four Winds Quilting
Large inventory of fabric, patterns,
and supplies for quilting and needlecrafts

1314 24th St. W, 406-694-1025
4windsquilting.com

Yarn Bar
Hard-to-find beautiful and high-quality
yarn Classes and open knitting groups

2909 2nd Ave. N, 406-534-4032
yarn.bar

75

BECOME A BIRDER
AT THE MONTANA AUDUBON CENTER

The Audubon Center is a gem of a wildlife preserve in Billings that straddles the line between nature and urban living. While predominantly a bird habitat and research center, the Audubon Center also has a visitor center with friendly naturalists available to share information about many local birds, animals, and plants. Outside, walking paths meander around the property and its many gardens. You'll notice there's even a nature-themed preschool on-site. If you're not a preschooler, don't worry—you can still expand your knowledge of nature. Classes and hands-on activities are offered throughout the year. Morning bird-watching strolls and full-moon night hikes are popular events for individuals and families. However you choose to experience the Audubon Center, you'll no doubt leave it feeling more appreciative and knowledgeable about the wildlife and plants that make the Yellowstone Valley so special.

7026 S Billings Blvd., 406-294-5099
mtaudubon.org/center

TIP

Go to Wild Birds Unlimited to get advice and supplies for attracting birds to your own backyard. The knowledgeable staff can show you how to turn your home into a bird feeding habitat. Wild Birds Unlimited frequently partners up with the Montana Audubon Society to host local events.

IMMERSE YOURSELF AMONG LEGEND AND VIEWS

AT SACRIFICE CLIFF

One of the most mesmerizing sections of scenery in Billings is a large sandstone outcrop bordering a curving section of the Yellowstone River. The sandstone height ranges from 200 to 500 feet tall with a nearly 90-degree drop off the plateau, from where you can gaze over a beautiful panoramic view of Billings. Sacrifice Cliff is an important spiritual place for Native Americans and has an intriguing backstory, or perhaps what's better referred to as a legend. Sacrifice Cliff is believed to be where two Crow warriors jumped to their deaths after returning home from a hunt or raid, only to find their families and tribe wiped out from smallpox. As with all legends, parts of the story are conflicting: some tell the legend as being more of a love story, while some believe the actual place of the jump was farther down the river. Regardless, looking at Sacrifice Cliff, you can imagine the torment the two warriors must have felt and the ensuing legend.

1100 Coburn Rd., 406-896-5013
blm.gov/visit/four-dances-srma

VISIT AN ART GALLERY
WITH AN INDEPENDENT SPIRIT

You won't find a supermarket inside Kirks' Grocery anymore. Today, the vacant space that was once selling food is now home to an indie art gallery, while continuing the previous name of the building. Kirks' Grocery is also the place for budding musicians, poets, comedians, and other performance-based artists to come together and create shows and community. The owner started the art gallery and cooperative after being inspired by European punk collectives. Art exhibits at Kirks' Grocery change frequently so you can check back every month or so and likely see new art on display. Want to be more involved? Membership is available for those who want an area in which to practice their craft. Another type of membership is available for those who just want to support the arts and also get a 10 percent discount off merchandise sold in the space.

2920 Minnesota Ave., 503-209-2394
kirksgrocery.com

PERUSE PUBLIC ART AND POETRY

Time and again Billings has turned into a canvas for artists to create beautiful and conversation-starting mural art. These murals are located all around Billings and feature local lore such as bison, mountains and rivers, and western scenes. We recommend starting your mural journey in downtown Billings with a visit to the building in which Jake's Restaurant is located, where you'll see a huge bison painted on the side of the building. The traffic signal boxes are also delightedly covered in artistic scenes. Not to be outdone by images, the art of the written word is also on display thanks to a collaboration between Healthy by Design and South Side Billings. Located around the South Side neighborhood are 18 sections of sidewalk that feature poetry written by residents and etched into the concrete, following the theme of "The Bright Side of the Tracks." You never know where a piece of public art will pop up next so keep an eye out for them as you explore Billings!

Downtown Billings Alliance:
downtownbillings.com/downtown-directory/art

South Side Poetry:
healthybydesignyellowstone.org/what-we-do/success-stories/creative-placemaking

LEARN ABOUT FRONTIER HISTORY AT THE YELLOWSTONE KELLY INTERPRETIVE SITE

Luther Sage "Yellowstone" Kelly was one of the original frontiersmen of Montana—he was a soldier, adventurer, and revered scout in Yellowstone Country. When he died in 1928, he requested to be buried on his beloved Rimrocks in Billings. In 2018, the city of Billings decided it was time to properly honor Yellowstone Kelly and built an interpretive site atop the Rimrocks with information boards about him and his importance to the region, as well as additional history of the Yellowstone River Valley. Located on the east side of Swords Rimrock Park, along the Chief Black Otter Trail, the interpretive site provides an incredible view of Billings. Looking over the immense valley from the same spot Yellowstone Kelly likely stood makes you imagine how it must have looked during his day.

TIP

Just down the trail from Yellowstone Kelly Interpretive Site is Boothill Cemetery, the cemetery for the old river town of Coulson back in the 1880s. The cemetery gets its name because rumor had it that bodies were buried still wearing their boots. You can still walk around it today to see old grave markers and read the informational plaques.

TAKE A WALK ON THE WILD SIDE

AT ZOOMONTANA

For living in such a small city, Billings's residents feel especially lucky to have such a wonderful, highly rated zoo. ZooMontana is open, spacious, and home to a wide range of animals. ZooMontana has several play areas with climbing and sliding equipment plus inside spaces with hands-on learning stations and question/answer placards. They have exotic animals like the kookaburra singing from its perch and tigers roaming their habitat, and animals that are native to the American West, such as a wolf pack and grizzly bears.

2100 S Shiloh Rd., 406-652-8100
zoomontana.org

TIP

The zoo grounds get in the holiday spirit each December thanks to Holiday Nights at ZooMontana. You won't be visiting the animals, but you'll get to wander amid over 10 million twinkling lights that transform the zoo grounds into a winter village wonderland. For an unforgettable experience, we recommend renting one of the cozy s'mores huts. Sleigh rides, Santa photo packages, and a variety of food and drinks are also available during Holiday Nights. holiday-nights.com

Scheels Ferris Wheel

SHOPPING AND FASHION

GET FITTED FOR AN HEIRLOOM-WORTHY COWBOY HAT

AT RAND'S HAT SHOP

It seems everyone wants to be a Montana cowboy these days thanks to the hit TV show *Yellowstone*. And as real cowboys know, not every cowboy hat is created equal. If you want to truly embrace the western aesthetic, the place to go in Billings is Rand's Custom Hats. What started 50 years ago as a small hat shop for local ranchers to purchase high-quality hats has progressed into a world-renowned store that has created cowboy hats for celebrities and anyone who wants a tailor-made hat of the highest quality. After custom measurements for the perfect fit, the hat is expertly molded, sanded, and hand-stitched. A custom cowboy hat from Rand's is going to set you back hundreds (and possibly thousands) of dollars, and there's usually a monthslong wait list. Still, it's worth it for a hat that feels comfortable all day and should last you a lifetime with proper care.

2205 1st Ave. N, 800-346-9815
randhats.com

TIP

Don't want to wait? Check out iwannahat.com where Rand's sells ready-to-wear cowboy hats that are created with the same craftsmanship and quality as their custom hats.

KICK UP YOUR HEELS
IN A PAIR OF COWBOY BOOTS FROM AL'S BOOTERY

You're in boot country when you're in Billings. Whether you prefer cowboy boots or hiking boots—or both—you'll find them at Al's Bootery. They've been selling boots in Billings since 1946, and with 5,000 boots in their inventory, you can comfortably outfit the whole family for the ranch or mountain trails. If you have a pair of old boots that you love, but they're falling apart, Al's Bootery is the place to go in Billings for shoe repair. Accessorize your well-heeled outfit with a fun piece from the Girl Ran Away with the Spoon jewelry line that Al's Bootery carries; it's known for its vintage silverware jewelry and is based out of Miles City. Also on display in the store, you'll find a boot believed to have been worn by the world's largest man, Robert Wadlow, who was eight feet eleven inches tall when he died in 1940.

1820 1st Ave. N, 406-245-4827
alsbootery.ccm

TIP

For the ladies: Canty Boots, a Montana-based line that specializes in unique, short western boots designed for women, can be found at the boutique gift shop downtown in the Northern Hotel, 19 North Broadway. cantyboots.com

GEAR UP FOR YOUR MOUNTAIN ADVENTURES

AT THE BASE CAMP

Shop local at the Base Camp, which is the place to go for outdoor enthusiasts looking for personalized service and high-quality products when shopping for outdoor recreation products. Owned by Montanans, the Base Camp specializes in outdoor gear and accessories, whether you're looking to buy or rent. Cross-country skiing, camping, fishing, snowshoeing—you name it, they've probably got the supplies and gear you need or can get it for you. They also sell apparel with brands like Patagonia, Cotopaxi, and Fjallraven. The footwear section includes brands from the likes of Merrell, Keen, and Chaco. The staff is friendly and knowledgeable about mountain gear and how to properly fit equipment. If you're needing a gift for the mountain or river lover in your life, the Base Camp has a fun selection of unique T-shirts, puzzles, journals, baby clothes, Montana-themed products, and more.

1730 Grand Ave., 406-248-4555
thebasecamp.com

TIP

The Base Camp is the local sponsor of the Banff Centre Mountain Film Festival, which shows films in the historic Babcock Theatre as part of the festival's worldwide tour each spring. arthousebillings.com/Banff

RIDE A FERRIS WHEEL
IN A SPORTING GOODS STORE

Come to shop and stay for the fun at Scheels Billings, a sporting goods store that helps bring fun and excitement in and out of its store. Step through the doors and you'll find a 65-foot-tall Ferris wheel, a 16,000-gallon fish aquarium, large displays of taxidermied wildlife, arcade games, and even an event space upstairs. Scheels will help enhance your sporting and outdoor lifestyle too, with an assortment of gear and clothing filling up the 220,000-square-foot building. As you might expect from the taxidermy and fish tank, hunting and fishing have prominent sections. You can also find running shoes, skis, bicycles, kayaks, sporting equipment, and so much more. If you're feeling hungry and thirsty after all that shopping and playing, head over to Ginna's Café & Coffee, located right on-site.

1121 Shiloh Crossing Blvd., 406-656-9220
scheels.com/store?StoreID=086

85

AWAKEN YOUR INNER CHILD WITH A STOP AT ACTION TOYS

It's hard to think of a more fitting store for southeast Montana than Action Toys, a unique toy store that specializes in toy tractors. A lot of toy tractors. The owner of Action Toys has a private collection of more than 4,000. While those tractors and other farm memorabilia may not be for sale, many of them are on display for you to see in the 4,400-square-foot retail space. If you're looking to start your own farm toy collection or in the market for a fun gift, Action Toys sells replicas of all types of farm equipment including the tractors that range from antique treasures for collectors to new-age pink tractors ready to delight every pastel-loving kid. Depending on inventory, you also may see ride-on toy tractors and trucks for sale. Whether you leave with a toy or not, you'll definitely start dreaming like a kid again as you gaze at the farm-inspired toys.

2274 SE Shiloh Rd., 406-651-8199
actionfarmtoys.com

PICK OUT A PIECE OF WESTERN ART OR DECOR
AT THE FRAME HUT

This custom frame shop isn't just for those looking to get a new setting for their favorite photograph or piece of art. The Frame Hut & Gallery is open to shoppers who want to absorb an artsy atmosphere in a welcoming and casual setting. The shop is filled with works from local artists and artisans, available for purchase. Many focus on nature and western themes. The Frame Hut helps to beautify your space beyond framing and art, with home decor, pottery, and small furniture available for purchase. Not sure how to assemble art in your home to create a personal and inviting space? They offer design consultation services for both home and office. The Frame Hut & Gallery has been in Billings for over 50 years and continues to evolve with home trends, framing techniques, and supporting local artists.

1430 Grand Ave., 406-245-9728
framehut.com

TIP

The Frame Hut carries art by lifelong Southeast Montana resident and artist Harry Koyama, who is known for colorful paintings of wildlife and the American West. To see more of Koyama's art, stop by his gallery in the Billings Historic District. 2509 Montana Avenue, 406-259-2261, harrykoyama.com.

PURCHASE A RIVER-ENGRAVED CUSTOM FLY BOX
FROM STONEFLY STUDIO

Love fly fishing and artisan creations? Then Stonefly Studio is a must-visit place for you in Billings. This little shop specializes in beautiful, handmade fly boxes with incredible wooden tops, laser engraved with your favorite river and its tributaries. The back of the fly box can be personalized with an inscription above a chosen engraving of artwork designed by a local artist. In addition, stainless steel flasks, coffee mugs, cribbage boards, and decorative signs are available for custom engravings. Stonefly Studio also specializes in custom-made wooden tables with a gorgeous blue resin used for the engraving on top. Making the store even more endearing is that it got its start because the owner, Daniel Mazel, made a fly box in the garage to replace one his son lost. He kept going with the craft and it eventually turned into a business that has become a family affair since Stonefly Studio opened over 15 years ago.

134 Regal St., 406-656-6326
stoneflystudio.com

BUY A BAG TO LAST A LIFETIME

AT RED OXX

Red Oxx's headquarters and manufacturing facility are right in Billings and have been since 1986. Started by a veteran and now run by his son, also a veteran, Red Oxx originally produced weightlifting accessories using military-grade materials. In the '90s, they focused on their luggage products and pivoted to embrace the burgeoning Internet, selling directly to consumers, all while continuing their dedication to durable materials and meticulous craftsmanship. Today, Red Oxx is known for the highest-quality nylon luggage, bags, and sporting gear still made in Montana. Customer service and working directly with consumers is important to the Red Oxx ethos, resulting in the credo "not sold at a store near you." Unless, that is, you're in Billings. Then you can visit their factory store and look at their products in person, which range from packing cubes and messenger bags to carry-on suitcases and the practically indestructible "railroad bags."

310 N 13th St., 888-733-6999
redoxx.com

TIP

Call ahead before going to the store and see if you can plan your visit with a factory tour, during which you'll learn more about how these bags are made and about Red Oxx's contribution to the local economy in Billings.

SAVOR SUMMER'S FRESHEST TASTES
AT THE FARMERS MARKET

Agriculture reigns supreme during the summer season in the Yellowstone Valley. Take advantage of all that local produce with a visit to the Yellowstone Valley Farmers Market that hosts over 60 vendors selling the fruits of their labor each week. The vendors come from all over Montana, though most food being sold is grown within a 120-mile radius of Billings. Some growers have been participating in the market since it first began in 1985! The Yellowstone Valley Farmers Market is held Saturday mornings in downtown Billings from mid-July to early October. In addition to produce, you can enjoy a breakfast item from a bakery vendor or hot lunch from one of the vendors that sell their ready-to-eat cuisine. Live music creates a festive atmosphere while you shop and eat.

Intersection of N Broadway and 2nd Ave. N, 406-855-1299
yvfm.org

TIP

Another farmers market to check out is the community-focused Healthy by Design Gardeners' Market, which aims to bring healthy and affordable produce to the South Park area of Billings from mid-June through early October. S 28th St. and 7th Ave. S, healthybydesignyellowstone.org/what-we-do/current-initiatives/gardeners-market

DISCOVER NEW TREASURES
AT A COUNTRY GENERAL STORE

Liberty and Vine is a country general store owned by born-and-raised Montanans. Located in a remodeled century-old brick warehouse in downtown Billings, the ambiance adds to the allure of this unique emporium where you never know what delights you'll find. The inventory changes daily so it's a fun place to frequent for gifts and decor for your home. Liberty and Vine is reminiscent of country stores commonly found throughout New England, and they even source some of their products from those country stores out east. Liberty and Vine pays close attention to its western roots, though. The store carries a wide range of "Made in Montana" products, from candy to jewelry. Additionally, you'll find an assortment of antiques, clothing, food items, and home decor. Really, though, the fun of this store is wandering around it with nothing particular in mind to buy, and seeing what treasures catch your eye.

2019 Montana Ave., 406-534-8667
libertyandvine.com

91

SEARCH FOR A PIECE OF MONTANA'S PAST
AT THESE ANTIQUE STORES

With a history of homesteading and country charm, Montana is a great place to go antique hunting, and two places in Billings make it fun and easy to do just that: Marketplace 3301 and Yesteryears Antique Mall. Both places have gorgeous, one-of-a-kind antiques, from furniture and decor to art and toys. Fashionistas will love that both stores have a vintage clothing section. The on-site coffee shop at Marketplace 3301 makes it easy to turn a quick stop into an all-day browsing session by providing an easy place to fuel up with caffeine and a snack. Yesteryears also has a coffee and hot chocolate counter with other snacks available for purchase; get a hot drink to sip on while you explore its three levels of vintage treasures. Both antique shops are located downtown, less than five blocks from each other. Happy antique hunting!

Marketplace 3301
3301 1st Ave. N, 406-281-8460
marketplace3301.com

Yesteryears Antique Mall
102 N 29th St., 406-256-3567
facebook.com/YesteryearsMT

GO ANTIQUE HUNTING

Broadwater Mercantile
1844 Broadwater Ave., 406-652-4590
facebook.com/broadwatermercantile

Junkyard 406
2135 Grand Ave., 406-294-2955
facebook.com/junkyard406

Montana Vintage Clothing
112 N 29th St., 406-248-7650
montanavintage.com

Oxford Hotel Antiques
2411 Montana Ave., 406-248-2094
oxford-hotel-antiques.business.site

Peddlers Station
645 Custer Ave., 406-245-0127
facebook.com/profile.php?id=100065524958377

R & R Trading
113 Northern Ave., Huntley, 406-348-2649
facebook.com/profile.php?id=100064115223859

Red Barn Antiques
11360 S Frontage Rd., Laurel, 406-628-7105
facebook.com/people/Red-Barn-Antiques-Collectables/100057450220023

92

EMBRACE AN ECO-CONSCIOUS WAY OF SHOPPING
AT FRAE

Frae Everyday Goods may sound ordinary, but it is actually a beautiful shop that feels like a breath of fresh air when you walk in. And Frae Everyday Goods is doing its part to keep that air fresh by selling natural, eco-friendly commodities and gifts with a goal of making it easier to shop locally and sustainably. You'll find biodegradable products and packaging, including environmentally safe soaps and cleaning products. Various items, such as the pantry supplies and skin-care regimens, are sourced right from local makers when possible in an effort to reduce the store's carbon footprint. Frae even has its own line of clothing made in Billings with a focus on conserving resources with minimal waste. The business continues that train of thought with a clothing alteration and repair service. If you're interested in doing it yourself, Frae hosts classes to teach you how to make various products to help reduce your own carbon footprint and waste.

Shiloh Commons, 115 Shiloh Rd., 406-200-7429
shopfrae.com

DISCOVER BEAUTIFUL CONTEMPORARY ART
AT TOUCAN

Beauty, uniqueness, and affordability flock together at Toucan, a contemporary art gallery, boutique, and custom framing shop that is all about beautiful things. Toucan has a variety of paintings, handblown glass, pottery, jewelry, and other mixed media creations for sale in a historic building on Montana Avenue that has been thoughtfully restored by the owners, and then filled with carefully curated art and artisan-crafted items, all from local and regional artists. The space has been used as an art gallery for decades and is the oldest building in Billings to still be used by an art gallery to this day. The owners want everyone to feel welcome and for Toucan to be a place shoppers can visit to experience and purchase delightful and intriguing contemporary art that speaks to them. Stationery, scarves, hats, and other accessories are also for sale, making it a great place to find a special gift for someone.

2505 Montana Ave., 406-252-0122
toucanarts.com

IMMERSE YOURSELF
IN THE LOCAL BOOK LOVERS COMMUNITY

This House of Books is an independent bookstore in downtown Billings that blends a love of books with community. This House of Books is a co-op, meaning its members have a stake in the bookstore and get discounts when shopping there. Add in the friendly staff and this is a bookstore where you'll want to frequently hang out. This House of Books makes it even easier to spend time there with special events, such as book signings and launches, poetry readings, story time for kids, and more literary-focused get-togethers. In addition, This House of Books hosts a game night every Thursday and a writing group meetup on Tuesdays. Adding to the homey atmosphere of This House of Books is the small tea shop in the back of the store where you can order a cup of tea and sit down with a good book or good friend at one of the tables in front of the tea counter.

116 N 29th St., 406-534-1133
thishouseofbooks.indielite.org

95

SHOP
FOR MONTANA'S EXQUISITE GEM— THE YOGO SAPPHIRE

A yogo sapphire is a prized Montana gemstone to add to a piece of fine jewelry. Yogo sapphires are known for their vivid cornflower-blue color and impeccable clarity. They are unique to Montana and only found in the Yogo Gulch within the Little Belt Mountain Range. Several Billings jewelers specialize in yogo sapphire jewelry and custom creations using yogos.

Goldsmith Gallery Jewelers is the place to head for variety. They have the largest selection of yogo sapphires in the entire country. If you have an heirloom piece or loose sapphire that you want to create into a custom piece of jewelry, Berkman Custom Jewelers can help you create just what you have in mind. Two other locally owned jewelers that are excellent sources for high-quality yogo sapphire jewelry and stones, including estate pieces, are Montague's Jewelers and Greenleaf's Jewelry.

Goldsmith Gallery Jewelers
903 Shiloh Crossing Blvd.
406-252-3662
goldsmithgalleryjewelers.com

Berkman Custom Jewelers
411 24th St. W
406-534-4755
berkmancustomjewelers.com

Montague's Jewelers
2810 2nd Ave. N
406-294-9370
montaguesjewelers.com

Greenleaf's Jewelry
312 8th St. W
406-245-7424
greenleafsjewelry.com

ADMIRE THE WORK
OF INDIGENOUS DESIGNERS AND ARTISANS

Buffalo Chips Indian Arts and Crafts has one of the best selections of Native American jewelry, artwork, and craft supplies in the region. Browse the store and select an already completed piece of art, beadwork, or jewelry to adorn yourself and home, all crafted by Indigenous artisans. Or get inspired to make your own art, accessories, or clothing; Buffalo Chips makes it easier thanks to a large selection of materials. Choose from strung hackles in an array of colors, and fabrics that feature Indigenous designs, patterns, and instructions; peruse an assortment of beads; and select just the right feathers, quills, and leather for regalia creations. They even specialize in one-of-a-kind engagement rings, and their expert staff can help you pick out the perfect piece. In addition to selling jewelry, Buffalo Chips has an on-site jewelry repair shop.

327 S 24th St. W, Ste. 2, 406-656-8954
buffalochipsindianart.com

TIP

To view Indigenous designers at the height of their profession, make plans to attend the Indigenous Fashion Gala at the Big Sky Indigifest this summer. In 2022, the Fashion and Art Gala was started in Billings as a way to showcase Indigenous fashion designers, makeup artists, hair stylists, and models. With plans to be an annual event that is part of the Big Sky Indigifest, the runway gala will feature over a dozen Indigenous designers from Montana and North America showcasing their designs live in front of an audience.

facebook.com/people/Big-Sky-Indigifest-Fashion-Gala-2023/100089417475270

97

HAVE FUN KIDULTING
AT THESE STORES

Want to feel like a kid again and play with a bunch of toys, model cars, and trading cards? Then jump on the "kidulting" trend and embrace the whims of your inner child by visiting one of Billings's niche hobby shops.

Central Hobbies: For the die-hard model hobbyist, it's a small but heavily stocked store that specializes in kits for model cars and motorcycles, boats and ships, planes, and trains. They are also well stocked with parts, paint, and other repair supplies you may need. 1401 Central Ave., 406-259-9004, centralhobbies.com

Keep It Alive Antiques and Collectibles: Not your typical antique shop—it's lined with superhero dolls and toys still in the box, perfect for toy collectors. Atari, PlayStation, VHS, and more nostalgia abounds. If you want to go back to your childhood and find your toys from the '80s and '90s, this is the place to go. 928 Broadwater Ave., 406-598-7692, facebook.com/keepitaliveanc

KAB Sports Cards and Collectables: Card collectors should head to KAB Sports Cards and Collectables which buys and sells cards ranging from professional sports to game cards like Pokémon and Yu-Gi-Oh. Deck boxes and sleeves are also sold so you can keep your collection pristine. 2059 Broadwater Ave., 406-702-1509, kabsportscards.com

98

GET YOUR HOLIDAY SHOPPING DONE EARLY

IN A FESTIVE SETTING

The Holiday Food and Gift Festival is a place where you can find a Christmas present for everyone on your list in just one day. Thousands of people flock to this festival held in MetraPark's Expo Center for one shopping-filled weekend each November. Admission is low and is highly discounted if you bring a nonperishable food item as a donation for the Billings Food Bank. More than 200 vendors are typically at this event selling a variety of unique products, yummy treats, and artisan gifts. The multitude of booths showcase soaps, T-shirts, skin care, children's books, pastries, oils, artwork, woodworking, jewelry, and so much more. Kids may not be excited to go shopping, but they will no doubt get excited when they see Santa at this festival. Entertainment by dance groups and other performers on stage adds to the festive atmosphere throughout the event.

308 6th Ave. N, 406-861-3931
holidayfoodandgiftfestival.com

99

GIVE SMILES
WITH A GIFT FROM THE JOY OF LIVING

The Joy of Living is one of our favorite places to find a gift for a friend or loved one. It's thoughtfully curated by the store's owner, who was inspired to open her own gift shop after visiting boutiques during a trip to Pier 51 in San Francisco. A bright space and friendly service await you, and the employees at The Joy of Living are happy to give you ideas on what to select if you're feeling stumped on that perfect gift. But we have to admit, we often leave with more items we keep for ourselves than those we are gifting! The Joy of Living has a variety of products, from candles and novelty books to locally made jewelry and high-quality leather accessories. The baby goods section of the store has adorable and unique finds for the littlest ones in your life. As the perfect finishing touch, The Joy of Living also offers free gift wrapping with your purchase.

1524 24th St. W, 406-294-1701
thejoyofliving.com

100

STEP OUT IN STYLE
AFTER SHOPPING AT THESE FINE STORES

Billings isn't just about the cowboy hats and boots. Step out in all the latest trends or find your own style at these fashion-forward boutiques in Billings.

Cricket: This carefully curated shop will help you be fashionable and classy all at once, with plenty of bags and jewelry items to accessorize your new outfit. Largest selection of Brighton jewelry and bags (and more) in Montana.

2814 2nd Ave. N, 406-259-3624, cricketclothingco.com

Neecee's: With fun colors and quality materials, Neecee's will have you shopping for comfort without sacrificing looking good, whether it's for work or play. Brands include the likes of Liverpool and Tommy Bahama.

1008 Shiloh Crossing Blvd., Ste. 2, 406-294-2014, neecees.com

RocHouse: Browse what's hip and happening in the fashion world at this trendy clothing store. Shop brand names like Blanc Noir, Trina Turk, James Peres, and Agolde.

1025 Shiloh Crossing, 406-652-9999, rochouse.mybigcommerce.com

Something Chic: Current fashion with a hint of western flair, located in downtown Billings. Personal shopping sessions and shopping parties are available to book, complete with bubbly to sip while you browse!

2818 2nd Ave. N, 406-702-4465, somethingchicclothing.com

THIRSTY
STREET
BREWING CO.

ACTIVITIES BY SEASON

SPRING

SUMMER

FALL

WINTER

SUGGESTED ITINERARIES

TAKE THE KIDS IN THE SUMMER

TAKE THE KIDS IN THE WINTER

WATER SPORTS IN SOUTHEAST MONTANA

RIMS AND TRAIL ADVENTURES

FOLLOW THE PATH OF HISTORY

THE WESTERN WAY OF LIFE

DATE NIGHT

OPTION 1

OPTION 2

GIRLS NIGHT

DAY TRIPS FROM BILLINGS

A SHORT STAY IN BILLINGS

INDEX